JEFF BEZOS

THE WORLD-CHANGING ENTREPRENEUR

CHRIS MCNAB

PICTURE CREDITS

Amazon: 16, 19, 24, 27, 32, 49, 59, 61, 62, 110, 128, 135, 136, 150, 164, 173, 179, 180
Getty: 104, 176

This edition published in 2022 by Arcturus Publishing Limited
26/27 Bickels Yard, 151–153 Bermondsey Street,
London SE1 3HA

AD006747UK

Printed in the UK

CONTENTS

INTRODUCTION

It seems safe to say, without the risk of creating a hagiography, that Jeff Bezos is one of the most extraordinary individuals of the modern age. Some caution goes with this claim. The biographer of any great public figure can be easily seduced into oversubscribing agency to all the twists and turns of their subject's story. Much of life, after all, is a pinball-like experience, bouncing between disconnected events and random decisions. Only with memory and retelling are these episodes stitched together into a clean narrative with direction and purpose. At the same time, it is easy to underplay the statistical possibility of success in a world of near-infinite human games – maybe, after all, this individual was simply the lucky one. In logical modelling, we call this error 'survival bias'. Here, the observer automatically selects rare high-achievers and attributes causation to all their moves on the chessboard, seeing their *actions* as the secret sauce to success. The problem is that the vast majority of individuals who *don't* achieve greatness are largely invisible; the fact that some might have taken almost identical actions but still failed isn't taken into account. Single causes largely beyond the entrepreneur's control – a parent who falls ill for a few months, a single misguided acquisition, a sudden legal threat, a fire at a warehouse – can initiate the destructive countdown that ultimately leads to bankruptcy and boarded-up windows. We as observers like to whistle while we pass this truly vast graveyard, preferring to focus on the encouraging signs of those few who soared to the heavens.

So, a biography of Jeff Bezos runs the risk of ignoring survival bias, not least because Bezos cut his entrepreneurial teeth at a truly distinctive time in world history. During the 1980s and 1990s, our planet began the rocket-ride of technological revolution, as the personal computer and the internet together began reshaping the fabric of the modern age, right down to the ways we behave as societies and think as individuals. Bezos was fortuitously born at just the right time to intersect with this moment, stepping aboard as the aircraft was taxiing out to the runway for take-off. Various other factors gave an advantage: a loving and academically encouraging family environment; exposure to stimulating ideas and technologies; connections built up at Princeton and in business. In many ways, Bezos' first two decades of life ensured that he sat in the equivalent of a planetary 'Goldilocks Zone', the optimal location for potential future prosperity.

But when we remind ourselves of the sheer scale of what Bezos has achieved, the normal equations applied to working out the success formula seem almost to melt away. On 5 July 2021, Jeff Bezos stepped down as the CEO of the company he had created, Amazon, Inc. At that point, if Bezos took a moment of pause to reflect on what he had created, what would he see? In a world of an estimated 24 million e-commerce companies, Amazon occupied the unchallenged summit, with an annual revenue of nearly $470 billion (a figure accurate for the full year of 2021). In fact, Amazon is in the Top 5 largest companies on the planet, jostling with the likes of Apple, Microsoft, Alphabet and Saudi Arabian Oil. Amazon truly became the 'everything store' Bezos intended it to be – at the time of writing this book, it is estimated that the company is offering the public about 12 million products stocked by Amazon itself, expanding to 350 million product lines when we include the contributions of Marketplace sellers. In 2021, Amazon Prime alone had 200 million paid members worldwide and in 2019, a peak year, Amazon received 2.79 billion visitors. Through Amazon, the public can buy everything from baked beans to medical supplies, chainsaws to camping tents, baby toys to high-fashion handbags. For huge swathes of the world's population, including the author, Amazon is literally the first click when it comes to buying almost anything. The success of the retail business has also grown for more than two million third-party sellers around the world who chose to sell in the Amazon store, many of which are small- and medium-sized businesses. These businesses account for roughly 60 per cent of sales in the Amazon store.

But under Bezos' rudder Amazon became so, so much more than an online shop on a massive scale. It is now present in bricks-and-mortar high-street stores, including revolutionary 'Just Walk Out' technology-enabled stores in which the customer doesn't even negotiate a checkout. Amazon Publishing now publishes its own books, and Amazon also provides the Kindle Direct Publishing (KDP) self-publishing service; official figures for the numbers of self-published KDP works are not available, but even by 2016 they were reported to be more than a million. Amazon Web Services (AWS) is the world's largest provider of cloud computing services (according to Statista data for 2021, it holds 33 per cent of the cloud computing market) and live streaming – a commercial entity that supplies the digital infrastructure to thousands of companies and government agencies and billions of transactions, and whose reach touches our daily lives in more ways than we might conceive. Amazon has become an internationally respected player in film and TV, producing original content through Amazon Studios (in March 2021, films released by Amazon Studios received 12 Oscar nominations) and more than 200 million Prime members streamed viewings of TV programmes in 2021. Millions of Amazon-produced electronic devices – Kindles, Fire Sticks, Echo smart speakers – sit in hands or homes. Amazon has vast subsidiaries and investments, in industries or markets such as satellites, autonomous vehicles and computer hardware.

If we need a further marker of Amazon's big bang expansion then we can point to the fact that when Amazon first launched in 1994 it used a domestic garage as its warehouse; today, it has hundreds of giant logistics facilities around the world and 1.3 million employees. Twenty-two countries have their own dedicated Amazon platforms (at the time of writing: United States, United Kingdom, Australia, Canada, China, France, Germany, India, Ireland, Italy, Japan, Mexico, Spain, Brazil, Netherlands, Egypt, Turkey, Singapore, UAE, Saudi Arabia, Sweden and Poland), but Amazon can reach customers in more than 100 other countries through its international direct shipping. Amazon is in our rooms and pockets, on our desktops, through our letterboxes, driving our businesses.

Attempting to summarize Amazon's scale and achievements is always a rather breathless activity, never quite fully conveying the scale of what is, after all, one of the biggest commercial success stories in all history, not just modern times. But what is extraordinary is that Amazon is no longer the only definer of Bezos' relentless achievements. In addition, he has built one of the world's leading space exploration programmes, Blue Origin, and personally travelled into space inside one of his own spacecraft.

He has created multi-billion-dollar philanthropic foundations, created a network of new schools, owns the *Washington Post*, has invested in hundreds of different companies, has sunk billions into technology R&D and, for good measure, is building a clock that ticks for 10,000 years.

All the above has famously brought Jeff Bezos untold riches. In July 2018, Bezos was named the 'richest man in modern history', when his net worth hit $150 billion – this rose to $200 billion in 2020. Bezos' wealth has become an obsessive lens through which the public views the man. (In an interesting aside, it should be noted that Jeff Bezos has not taken any additional Amazon shares since the company's founding; the growth in his wealth has largely rested upon the increase in the value of those shares.) But the personal wealth of Jeff Bezos, as I hope this biography will show, is in many ways a poor metric by which to measure his success. Far better is to concentrate our focus on *how* he made his mark on this planet. How does he think? How does he innovate? How does he manage teams, time, money and risk? By exploring such questions, and many more, we see Bezos' wealth more as an outcome than as a goal, which is largely the way Bezos sees it himself. Once we move past the wealth, we are more open to view the lessons of an extraordinary life.

CHAPTER 1

ENTRY POINT

The Greek philosopher Aristotle once famously said, 'Give me a child until he is 7 and I will show you the man.' Subsequent centuries of science and psychology have largely corroborated this observation, demonstrating that a child's early-years environment lays the solid foundations, or not, of their subsequent intellectual and emotional development. Even in extreme youth, however, there are points of decision and redirection. In the case of one young man destined for greatness, we can identify a clear fork in the road at the age of four.

THE START

Jeff Bezos was born on 12 January 1964, in Albuquerque, New Mexico. His mother, Jacklyn Gise, was just 16 when she fell pregnant, still a sophomore at high school. As her tender years suggest, the pregnancy was the unplanned outcome of a youthful romance. Jackie (as she is known) had fallen for one Theodore (Ted) Jorgensen, a charismatic 18-year-old and school senior. Ted's family hailed from Chicago, although he could trace his ancestry back to Danish immigrant grandparents. The Jorgensen family moved to Albuquerque when Ted was still in his single-digit years and it was there Jackie encountered him – a teenager straining against his early adult years. The attraction might have been assisted by Ted's unusual skill as a unicyclist – no mere pastime, but rather a professional pursuit. Ted had considerable talent atop the single wheel, whether riding backwards, on a high wire, or in formation with the other members of his performing troupe, the Unicycle Wranglers, appearing in shows, fairs, circuses (including major branded circuses such as the Ringling Brothers and Barnum & Bailey) and other events across the United States.

With the unexpected pregnancy, the high-school romance between Jackie and Ted ran full-force into the wall of reality. Jackie at least had the security of a solid family, one that would also have a seminal intellectual and emotional importance in the life of her son. Her father Lawrence Preston Gise, affectionately known as 'Pop' to family and close friends, and her mother Mattie gave Jackie an emotional bedrock. Lawrence was a professional man, a regional director in the United States Atomic Energy Commission (AEC), the organization formed in 1946 to take control of American atomic science research and facilities. Mattie's family had a 25,000-acre ranch near Cotulla, Texas. Three elements brought to the table by his maternal grandparents – loving nature, scientific interest and a physical space to explore – would become shaping forces on the young Jeff as he made his way through to adulthood.

For the teenage Jackie and Ted, life started throwing up problems, for which Jackie found imperfect but practical solutions. Before their child arrived, they married, although the legalities associated with their age meant they did so in Juàrez, Mexico, Jackie's family providing the financial means to make the journey. In Albuquerque, the couple rented a small apartment, the first home to their new arrival, Jeffrey Preston Jorgensen. The boy came into an environment characterized by the tensions of young people forced to adopt the trappings of serious adulthood before their time. Money was almost inevitably tight, despite financial assistance from Jackie's family. Ted's unicycling profession proved incompatible with his new responsibilities and he ended up grinding through a series of low-paid jobs, plus some failed attempts at furthering his educational status. The writing was on the wall – Jackie ended up moving back home with her parents and she filed for divorce when Jeff was just 17 months old. Thus the two separated, and Ted drifted out of Jeff's life for good.

Ted Jorgensen died in 2015, at the age of 70. Across his life, his literal and mental distance from Jeff had been profound. He was tracked down in 2012 by journalist Brad Stone, who found Ted running a bicycle-repair shop in Arizona. Almost inconceivably, he had no idea of the path his son's life had followed. Upon learning the truth, he expressed regret for and recognition of his failings as a young man and had no desire to reimpose himself on his grown son's life.

For Jackie, however, her time was now refocused on family-supported efforts to bring up her young son. Despite her situation, Jackie would from the outset consistently prove her capability as a protective (but not overly so) and determined mother, dedicated to the well-being and advancement of her boy. Through Jeff's growth years, she fanned the flames of her son's interests, fought his corner, believed in his capacities. While we should avoid any suggestion of biographical predestination, in many ways it is difficult to imagine Jeff's life having the same prodigious outcomes had he not had such a redoubtable and loving mother.

But she would not raise Jeff alone. An uptick in Jackie's fortune came when she started dating again, this time one Miguel 'Mike' Bezos. Miguel was a Cuban immigrant, one of 14,000

A young and smartly dressed Jeff Bezos poses with his mother, Jacklyn Bezos. Jacklyn was just 16 when she fell pregnant with Jeff and would remain a stable and devoted presence throughout his childhood.

unaccompanied Cuban children aged between 6 and 18 who were brought over to the United States to escape their parents' fears of life under the revolutionary regime of Fidel Castro. This movement was code-named Operation *Pedro Pan*, and it brought a tide of confused, scared, Spanish-speaking youth washing on to US shores, the children funnelled into large settlement camps and instructional centres. Miguel, as with all the children, had been separated from his parents, although the connection with family was partly maintained when he met up with his cousin, also an immigrant, and the two became inseparable. Much of the acclimation work for *Pedro Pan* was run by the Catholic Church, and Miguel and his cousin were fortunate that they came under the enlightened discipline of Father James Byrnes, who ran the Case de Sales home for 21 boys at 1300 Broom Street in Wilmington, Delaware. Byrnes ensured that all the children under his care were educated at the local Salesianum School, had a structured existence, and felt a sense of belonging and worth. The old truism 'What goes around comes around' is apt here. In June 2021, the Salesianum School in Wilmington – the evolution of the original home – received a $12 million endowment from Miguel and Jackie (shareholders in Amazon), $10 million of which was to go towards funding a total of 24 full scholarships, under the appropriately titled 'Rev. James P. Byrnes, OSFS Scholarship'. Regrettably, James Byrnes himself had died in 2020.

Miguel met Jackie when he took a part-time job as a clerk in the Bank of New Mexico, supporting himself as he attended the first year of study at the University of Albuquerque in the mid-1960s. Jackie was there holding down a job as a bookkeeper. Romance blossomed across overlapping shifts and struggling communications (Miguel was still working on his English), building up to their marriage in April 1968.

Miguel, or 'Mike' as he became known, would prove to be a blessing for both Jackie and her son. He was a hard-working and responsible husband and father, with a determined work ethic and an aptitude for engineering that landed him a good job with the ExxonMobil oil company, a position that involved the family moving to Houston, Texas. Mike had a scientific and questioning mindset, one that fostered debate, analysis, scrutiny and a submission to logic. Given his background in Cuba, furthermore, he was also passionate about the civil liberties and freedom of speech offered by the United States – an antipathy towards excessive government intervention rubbed off on Jeff (Stone 2018: 185), a fact that possibly goes some way to explaining his sometimes prickly relationship with government authorities and figures. Wanting stability for his new family, Mike adopted Jeff, whose surname now changed from Jorgensen to Bezos. In the immediate years after their wedding, Jackie and Mike brought into the world two more children, Christina and Mark. For Jackie, the early unsettled years were behind her and Jeff was now part of a loving and secure family.

MODELS FOR MANHOOD

The talents and capacities of some entrepreneurs emerge in a slow-burn fashion later in life, having shown little indication of their potential during their childhood. Jeff Bezos is not one of those people. From the outset, he seemed intent on forging a different, high-energy path from those around him, something his mother noticed early on. Jackie remarked in interview that when Jeff was two-and-a-half years old, she took him to a playground. He climbed on to a spinning boat ride along with a host of other children, but while the other kids shrieked with joy at the physical movement, Jeff was mentally focused on the mechanics of the ride itself, studiously and quietly watching the ride's cable and pulley system in action. Shortly after, he also attempted to take his crib apart with a screwdriver – clearly the boy was fascinated by how the world was put together, and mechanically understood that he could shape that world through his own efforts.

Jeff's school years foreshadowed many of the characteristics that would power his later professional career and the formation of Amazon, supported by the fact that he had the opportunity to thrive in educational institutions with high standards of teaching. At the Montessori pre-school he attended before elementary school, teachers noted that the infant Bezos was unusually attentive and focused, gripped by the task at hand and determined to see it through to completion. In the River Oaks Elementary School, where he was educated from 4th to 6th grades, he was placed on the Vanguard gifted and talented programme. His exceptionalism took several clear directions in both aptitude and interest. He showed a strong appetite for anything to do with technology, not least computers. In the 1970s, publicly accessible computers were still a rarity, most of the machines being confined to industry and defence. Yet River Oaks had the good fortune of connections to a local company with spare mainframe capacity, which it lent to the school and that the children could access through a teletypewriter. In comparison to the technology we know today, the system was

Jeff Bezos' first encounter with computers was via a teletypewriter at the River Oaks school. He was hooked on digital possibilities from the outset.

almost prehistorically clunky, but the interaction between machine and mainframe fascinated Bezos, not least the way that the system could be programmed to produce new outputs.

Bezos' burgeoning interest in technology found a natural corollary in all matters related to space. The *Star Trek* series, which premiered in 1966, was a constant inspiration to play and thought. Bezos and his friends would enact or create *Star Trek* scenes with all the fidelity of childhood imagination, with cardboard tasers and one child taking the role of the starship *Enterprise*'s verbal computer. This computer, with its ability to handle naturalistic voice inputs, would linger in Bezos' mind, an early seed later flowering into the Amazon Echo speaker and the Alexa virtual assistant. (In 2016, Bezos actually made a cameo as an alien Starfleet official in the movie *Star Trek Beyond*, fulfilling a life-long dream to be an actual, albeit theatrically fleeting, part of the *Star Trek* franchise.)

Education was not the only space that enabled Bezos to explore the world and hone his talents. In 1968, his beloved Pop had resigned from the AEC, thereafter spending more time at the family ranch. Jeff would play out much of his summer vacation months there, finding both a space to explore and a formative influence in the person of his maternal grandfather. Pop was a true countryman – self-reliant, hardy, rigorously practical. Any task on the ranch, from castrating bulls to repairing complex farm machinery, was tackled with creative thinking, improvisation and self-education, rather than automatically reaching for the phone to call for outside help (Pop also hated the unnecessary waste of money). Bezos shared in the ranch work and was encouraged to develop the same qualities of self-reliance and adaptability, the ranch becoming a wide-open, sunny space in which the young boy could 'invent and wander' (to use the title of a future collection of Bezos' writings) in a hands-on fashion.

But Pop also encouraged Bezos' evident intellectual interests, taking the boy on trips to the local library to broaden his mind, including through reading some of the greats of science fiction, such as Isaac Asimov and Robert Heinlein. There is an unbroken continuity between Bezos' childhood fascination in space and science fiction and his own flight into space on 20 July 2021, aboard the *New Shepard* rocket built and launched by his own aerospace/space exploration company, Blue Origin. Indeed, it can be plausibly argued that all Bezos' revolutionary entrepreneurial efforts, centrally the founding and stratospheric expansion of Amazon, have been in service of fulfilling his visions of space exploration and the possibilities of humans one day living and thriving on different planets. In 2018, *Wired* reporter Steven Levy secured an interview with Bezos to talk about his Blue Origin venture. A precondition of the interview was that Levy would watch a 30-minute documentary first broadcast in 1975, called 'Roundtable', in which Harold Hayes interviewed astrophysicist Gerard O'Neill and science-fiction writer Isaac Asimov. The interview (still available on YouTube) gave two great minds the opportunity to lay out visions for life beyond this world, including O'Neill's idea that Earth could one day became a pristine recreational park, visited by a humanity that had been shipped out to live on colonies in space. Exposure to this idea, as we shall see, has held an abiding fascination for Bezos, with the possibility of being a realizable goal. A later girlfriend of Bezos, Ursula Werner, remarked in interview that she felt Bezos also aspired to be a billionaire because that was the only way in which he would get to have his own space station (Stone 2018: 193).

Positive adult role models abound in Bezos' early years, but Pop was certainly central. One story, revealed by Bezos himself at a commencement address at Princeton, illustrates how his grandfather was not just concerned with fostering his grandson's intellectual strength, but also his moral compass. During a caravanning trip with Pop and Mattie, Bezos breezily informed his grandmother, who was a smoker, that he had calculated her smoking would reduce her life by nine years. Mattie, who was actually engaged in a fight against cancer, burst into tears. Pop took the child to one side and quietly but firmly gave him a crucial life lesson: 'Jeff, one day you'll understand that it's harder to be kind than be clever.' This motif of kindness underpinning cleverness is one that Bezos would frequently evoke in his speeches in later life; it clearly struck a chord.

Alongside his academic and cultural interests, Bezos involved himself to a degree in school sports, particularly baseball and football. By all accounts he was not the finest player at either sport, but he was competitive and committed, and he also brought a powerful memory and a native instinct for systems analysis to the game. At recruitment stage for the football team, for example, he was not automatically the strongest prospect, only just squeaking through the weigh-in. Yet two weeks later the coach gave him the role of defensive captain because he could remember all the plays and he could also mentally map all the positions of the opposing players.

When Bezos was 13, new work opportunities arose for his adoptive father, and the family moved out to Pensacola, Florida.

The physical move did not break the strong academic trajectory that Bezos had already established, and he was put on his new school's gifted programme, one year ahead of schedule. His teenage years showed an accelerating interest in all matters relating to technology and engineering. His theoretical study found practical expression in many exploratory projects, realized through modified home appliances or kit purchased at the local Radio Shack. A Hoover was thus transformed into a hovercraft. Alarm systems of various types and triggers popped up in the house, causing some trepidation for parents and siblings as they moved cautiously around their own home. An open umbrella, its fabric replaced by tin foil, became an experiment in solar cooking. It was clear that Jeff was not a child interested only in book learning; knowledge had to come alive in real-world expression.

Two years after the move to Florida, the family relocated once again, this time to Dade County, Miami, where Jeff attended school in Palmetto Bay. Jeff maintained his streak of inquisitive excellence, fuelled by a capacity for relentless hard work that teachers and fellow students found remarkable, and doubtless occasionally intimidating. He found new friends and challenges in the school's science and chess clubs, and he also attended the University of Florida's residential Student Science Training Program, which offered school students advanced learning in fields related to the sciences, engineering and computer technology. His abilities acted as a magnet for educational awards. These included not just repeated awards for best student in science and maths, but he also won a National Merit Scholarship in 1982. The year proved to be a fruitful one for Bezos, as he was also declared winner of the Silver Knight Award, a national scheme run since 1959 by the *Miami Herald* to award high-school seniors for exceptional academic performance.

During his later teenage years, Bezos began to reveal entrepreneurial leanings that ultimately never left him. Partly these were inspired by a revelation about what he *didn't* want to do in life. Famously, when he was 16 (in 1980), he took a job in McDonald's over the summer, working as a grill man in the

Homestead High's salutatorians are Chris Mueller and Tom DePlonty.

Killian

Michelle Sernaker, 17, first in a class of 749, will attend Massachusetts Institute of Technology and study engineering.

Sernaker won her school's French award and is one of three Dade students to win a corporate-sponsored National Merit Scholarship.

Sernaker

"I sort of wanted to be valedictorian the whole time. I couldn't have done it if I hadn't worked toward it," she said.

Salutatorian is **Joanne Kirk**.

Jeffrey Bezos, 18, first in a class of 680, will study electrical engineering and business administration at Princeton University.

He wants to build space hotels, amusement parks, yachts and colonies for two or three million people orbiting around the earth.

Bezos

"The whole idea is to preserve the earth," he said. His final objective is to get all people off the earth and see it turned into a huge national park.

Bezos won the Silver Knight winner in science and is a National Merit Scholar. He has won his school's Best Science Student award for the past three years

Please turn to BEST / 24

Sunday, June 20, 1982   w   The MIAMI HERALD   25

This brief profile of an 18-year-old Jeff Bezos in the Miami Herald *newspaper (20 June, 1982) illustrates how future visions of space were central to his thinking by his teenage years.*

back of the shop, making hundreds of burgers under the rush of customers. He didn't warm to the menial work, but he did learn some business lessons through direct observation, particularly about how speed could be obtained from automating processes. He watched the ways that orders, buzzers, friers and various other machines were choreographed into a ruthlessly efficient process designed to remove any barriers between the customers ordering their food and receiving it in their hands. In later interviews, he also explained that McDonald's taught him crucial early lessons about customer service and customer focus.

As invaluable as the experience at McDonald's was, when the following summer vacation came around he was determined not to return to the kitchen. Instead, and with considerable ambition, he created a ten-day summer-camp learning programme for 4th–6th graders, known as the DREAM Institute, which he would develop and run. Note that he was not offering some quaint childish effort – he was charging $600 per child, and eventually six people signed up to the event (although two of them were his own brother and sister). Much about Bezos' outlook was buried in the title of the summer camp: 'DREAM' stood for Directed Reasoning Method, a vision of intelligence being strapped to purposeful goals. The curriculum for the camp was a mix of literature, science and engineering – a polymath approach that he would later incorporate into the skills composition of his own companies. So the students on the course would find themselves one moment reading and discussing Tolkien's *Lord of the Rings* and Dickens' *David Copperfield* and the next moment finding out about black holes or the Apple II computer (the machine Bezos was using at this time), or about theories of interstellar space travel. In the flyer Bezos created to persuade parents to sign up their children, he explained that he would foster 'the use of new ways of thinking in old areas'.

Given the cumulative excellence Bezos had displayed throughout his education, and his emerging leadership skills, it was little surprise when he took the podium as the high-school valedictorian at the end of his school years. His speech married his love of all things space with a soaring youthful ambition, explaining to the young audience his dream of freeing humanity from its dependence upon this planet by establishing colonies out in space. Looking back, what might have seemed delusional fantasy in most other teenagers now appears to be a focused objective in the life of Jeff Bezos.

FROM UNIVERSITY TO WORK

The next step for Bezos following school was Princeton University, to which Bezos gained early entry on account of his school record and awards such as the Silver Knight. He enrolled in the elite Electrical Engineering and Computer Science (EECS) programme, Bezos being one of just 20 students to be accepted, with the aim of graduating with a Bachelor of Science in Engineering (BSE) degree. At this time, the BSE degree at Princeton held engineering and computer science as two specialities under one major. Within a year of his graduation, these two subjects were separated into their own degree majors. The fact that Bezos took a multidisciplinary approach to his subject, however, can only have worked in his favour when he came to set up Amazon, where he would be faced by technical problems that ranged from warehousing and distribution efficiency through to the complexities of online ordering and marketing in a period when the internet was still nascent.

Junior Jeff Bezos: the future scientist hopes to follow his flies into space someday. Photo by Barry Carothers

Bezos' ideas for future anything but earthbound

By J.L. WEINSTEIN

He wants to send flies into space; he has fixed everything from a windmill in Texas to a binary electronics system in Miami; he is President of Phi Beta Chi and past president of JETS; and he was first runner-up for the Miami Herald Grand Award in science at Dade County Youth Fair Science Fair.

Junior Jeff Bezos is obviously not the average student.

The National Space and Aeronautics Administration (NASA) and its Space Shuttle Student Involvement Program selected Bezos as one of the top 200 young scientists in the nation for his project, "The Effect of Zero Gravity on the Common Housefly."

For this, he and his faculty advisor Jeanna Ruel, have won an all-expense paid trip to the Marshall Space Flight Center, located in Huntsville, Alabama. This Space Flight Center is NASA's main research complex.

Bezos's idea calls for the sending of 9 cages of 75 houseflies each aboard the space shuttle. "My original idea," says Bezos, "was to find out whether zero gravity would reduce the aging process."

On the eighth and ninth of April, Bezos attended the Florida State Science Fair in Bradenton, Florida where he received a superior rating and the second place award

in physics for his project "The Effects of Ultrasonics on Air Friction."

Last summer he attended the Governors Program for Physics.

Bezos, who is a member of Spanish National Honor Society, Social Science Honor Society, Mu Alpha Theta, English Honor Society, and Phi Beta Chi, along with the Junior Engineering and Technological Society (JETS) and the Spanish Club plans on pursuing a career as a "Space Entepreneur."

Bezos says "The earth is finite, and if the world economy and population is to keep expanding, space is the only way to go." As a "space entepreneur," he would "construct solar power satellites that would make the world peaceful and affluent through abundant, cheap energy."

Last summer, Bezos attended the Governors Program for Physics, but most of his summers are spent at his grandfather's 2,000 acre ranch in Texas fishing and rounding up cattle on horseback.

Bezos says that the 3 people he admires most are "Bejamin Franklin, because he could do so many things well, Thomas Edison, because of his inventive mind, and Walt Disney, because of his ability to make people see his dreams."

This article in a local Miami paper captures the early exceptionalism of Jeff Bezos. Note how Bezos is quoted as wanting to be a 'space entrepreneur' – as the writer acknowledges, 'Jeff Bezos is obviously not the average student.'

While it can be superficially encouraging for lesser mortals (the author included) to read of billionaire entrepreneurs who dropped out of the college system to begin their ascent, Bezos was not one of those individuals. Indeed, his self-driven and competitive nature meant that he grasped university education with every intention to excel. He graduated in 1986 *summa cum laude* ('with the highest distinction') with a 4.2 Grade Point Average (GPA) – in terms of academic performance, this placed Bezos in the top 3 per cent of graduates. But elevated academic performance wasn't achieved at the expense of social involvement. His perpetual fascination with space matters continued – he became the president of the Princeton chapter of Students for the Exploration and Development of Space (SEDS), an international student organization dedicated, as its current website explains, to 'fostering the development of future leaders and contributors in the expanding space industry'. Bezos was also a member of the Phi Beta Kappa society, the oldest (founded in 1776) of the United States' national honorary scholastic societies; access to the Princeton chapter was only open to the highest-ranking tenth of students in their senior year of study. Similarly, Bezos was elected to the Tau Beta Pi Association, a national engineering honour society founded in 1885, whose doors opened only for those in the loftier tiers of academic ability. Packing further memberships into his university career, Bezos was a member of the Quadrangle Club (the 'Quad'), one of 11 'eating clubs' at Princeton. The eating clubs were essentially private dining and social clubs, each located in large mansion houses on Prospect Avenue (the Quad is located at number 33). Alumni of the Quad included senators, governors, ambassadors, judges, high-ranking military personnel and influential writers.

Bezos has retained a strong connection to Princeton, delivering addresses to students and faculty. His first-rate education doubtless gave his mind a technical reach that would later come in useful. Yet the greatest impact on Bezos of his Princeton education might have been a clarification about the nature and limits of talent. When he commenced university study, his original intention was to pursue theoretical physics as a path, but witnessing the soaring mathematical minds of some of the other students, particularly a gifted Sri Lankan called Yasantha Rajakarunanayake, led to a revelatory refocus. One day, Bezos and a friend, a highly capable physics student, were wrestling with an advanced mathematical problem and after hours of effort they were still no nearer to finding the solution. So they asked Rajakarunanayake, who had a truly exceptional mathematical brain, if he could help. In short order, Rajakarunanayake unpacked and solved the problem, producing three pages of detailed notes in the process. On 13 September 2018, Bezos gave an interview at the Milestone Celebration Dinner at the Economic Club of Washington in Washington DC, in which he explained the significance of what had just happened:

> That was an important moment for me, because that was the very moment when I realized I was never going to be a great theoretical physicist. I started doing some soul searching. In most occupations, if you're in the 90th percentile, you're going to contribute. In theoretical physics, you gotta be one of the top 50 people in the world, or you're really not helping out much.

Bezos had learned an age-old lesson – play to your strengths. He also understood that people are wired in different ways, and some can be exceptional for a fraction of the effort it would take others to achieve the same level of ability, if they could at all. Bezos' subsequent hiring and firing dynamic at Amazon – searching for the very best and brightest minds and rejecting those who couldn't accelerate Amazon quickly enough – is a reflection of this insight into human resources. Recognizing that theoretical physics was a field in which he could not stand out, he therefore changed his major and also, according to an interview with *Wired* magazine in 1999, decided that he was going to dedicate himself to succeeding in business. Though Bezos was unlikely to have realized it in 1985, Princeton introduced him to a new technology that would come to define not only Bezos' future, but the future of the planet – the internet.

INTO BUSINESS

Given his academic achievements and the prestigious university and social connections he had forged at Princeton, and the rising influence of computer technology on almost every field of science, business, finance and government, Bezos graduated as a highly employable individual. He received several immediate job offers, including from Intel (then holding a dominant lead in microprocessor production for the burgeoning personal computer [PC] market), Bell Labs and Andersen Consulting. For Bezos, however, his first major job came with a fast-growing financial telecommunications start-up called Fitel. Here was exactly the type of company in which the restlessly ambitious and innovative Bezos could find an initial intellectual home and financial self-sufficiency. The company had been founded in 1985 by academic mathematicians and scientists Graciela Chichilnisky and Geoffrey

Heal. Together, they developed an automated financial trading and settlement system called Equinet, which enabled PCs to connect to large-scale financial databases for faster and more responsive real-time trading. Here, Bezos was treated to an object lesson in what the internet could become when it was plugged into a source of valuable information and a direct customer need. He also saw how technology could produce massive efficiency savings over previous system models – using Equinet, the user could enter, confirm, settle and record a financial transaction, and also do it with complete data encryption. The proof of the system was demonstrated by Fitel's rapid growth, and by the time Bezos joined the company it had offices in New York, London and Tokyo.

From the start, Bezos impressed his new bosses with his problem-solving mindset and his ability to put in long and purposeful work hours. He became the head of development and the director of customer service; it is hard to think of two better positions in which Bezos could gain experience relevant to the foundation and early growth of Amazon. He also showed his ability to lead, variously running the London and New York offices. A key factor in Bezos' success was that he did not suffer from the introversion common to the world of computer engineering, a tendency that prevented many talented computer engineers from moving out of shadowy programming rooms into the leadership spotlight. Bezos certainly did not have a typical personality type. He was ruthlessly inquisitive, fanatically hard-working, awkward at times, but he had a crowning ability to focus on achieving a goal and then design both the effort and the system to achieve that goal. He was, and remains, stubbornly resistant to the idea that something is impossible.

The job with Fitel was the first in a series of Wall Street tech roles Bezos went through in the late 1980s and early 1990s. His next job, from 1988–90, was with the Bankers Trust Company in New York. Again, the role was at the intersection between finance and computerization. Given that Bezos was only in the company for two years, his rise up the ranks was steep, summiting in February 1990 when he was made the youngest ever vice president of the company. The job further acclimatized Bezos to handling huge volumes of trade, more than $250 billion of assets during the time he was there, through computer networks.

The next evolution in Bezos' career, however, would be a truly significant stepping stone on the path to creating Amazon. In 1988, David Elliot Shaw, formerly an assistant professor of computer science at Columbia University, established hedge-fund company D. E. Shaw & Co (aka DESCO). This would become one of the most innovative players on Wall Street, although its efforts to keep

Jeff Bezos stands aside his adoptive father, Mike Bezos, a Cuban immigrant who made a success of life and family in the United States.

its work, technology and client portfolios deliberately low-key led to James Aley in *Fortune* magazine labelling it in 1996 as the 'most intriguing and mysterious force on Wall Street'. At the time that article was published, DESCO had 300 employees, about $600 million in gross capital, and a trading volume equal to about 5 per cent of the entire New York Stock Exchange. Back in 1990, when Bezos joined the company, it was significantly smaller, but was already a force to be reckoned with.

Like Bezos, Shaw was driven by the potential of the internet, and had developed bespoke quantitative trading software that plugged into high-speed networks, the algorithms in the software accelerating the speed of trading and the identification and exploitation of opportunities. In the *Fortune* interview, Shaw himself explained that 'Our goal is to look at the intersection of computers and capital, and find as many interesting and profitable things to do in that intersection as we can.' Shaw became known as 'King Quant'.

The idea of a small, nimble, tech-driven company outperforming and outwitting older, bigger players was very compelling to Bezos, but there were other elements of the DESCO culture that would later manifest themselves in Amazon. The corporate culture was highly informal, with employees working in their leisure wear, but at the same time it was a place for hard workers, people who were driven to innovate and excel. Rather than concentrating on the recruitment of financiers, the company hired a high percentage of scientists and engineers, people who had cutting-edge knowledge of different fields of technology and innovation, and who could bring that knowledge to bear with fresh eyes on the system challenges of financial trading. The environment was intellectually demanding. At interview, candidates would be asked questions such as 'How many fax machines are there in America?', to see how they approached a problem by deduction and calculation rather than by mere memory or a pre-prepared answer.

Here was a place where Bezos felt both comfortable and challenged. His legendary capacity for long hours of work quickly manifested itself; he even kept a rolled-up sleeping bag next to his desk so that he could sleep in the office when it was simply too late to travel home. By 1993, he was running the options trading group based in Chicago and oversaw the company's entry into the 'third-market business', in which investors trade securities on an over-the-counter basis rather than going through an exchange, and thus saving the exchange's commissions placed on the trade. By 1992, Bezos was a senior vice president in the company. As at Bankers Trust, he was the youngest person in the company's history to hold this position.

Another significant gain from his time of working in DESCO was personal, not professional. MacKenzie Scott Tuttle was born on 7 April 1970 in San Francisco, California. In contrast to Jeff Bezos, the man she would later meet and marry, MacKenzie leaned heavily towards the creative arts, particularly fiction writing. She wrote her first manuscript, *The Book Worm*, when she was just six years old. The compulsion for writing continued through her teenage years, and such was her talent that after graduating from Hotchkiss School in Lakeville, Connecticut in 1988, she went on to take a bachelor's degree in English from Princeton University. One of her tutors, the great novelist Toni Morrison (winner of the Nobel Laureate in Literature in 1993), later remarked that MacKenzie was 'one of the best students I've ever had in my creative writing classes'. MacKenzie would work as a research assistant on Morrison's *Jazz* (1992), a critically acclaimed novel. In later life, she would also write two novels and several non-fiction titles.

That was in the future though. On graduation from Princeton, she went to work for DESCO as an administrative assistant. It was there that she met Bezos, who eventually became her direct manager. The attraction between them was rapid and mutual. MacKenzie was particularly taken by Bezos' powerful and whole-hearted laugh, a feature of Bezos' character noted by many other commentators as one of his most energizing and disquieting features. The attraction flowered into an office romance, which in turn led to an engagement three months after their first date, then a wedding in September 1993 in West Palm Beach, Florida.

DESCO was undoubtedly a place in which Bezos was flourishing, professionally and personally. It was also an environment in which Bezos, Shaw and other fertile minds could discuss future innovations, particularly related to the internet. One of the ideas knocked around was to create a free e-mail service, financially supported by advertising. DESCO was not the only company exploring this avenue. Hotmail was commercially launched on 4 July 1996 by entrepreneurs Sabeer Bhatia and Jack Smith, but in December 1997 it was sold to Microsoft for a reported $400 million. Yahoo! Mail was launched in October 1997, with both services providing email access through a standard web browser, rather than bespoke software. (Gmail would come much later, launched in 2004.) In May 1996, DESCO provided the equity capital and headquarters building for Juno Online Services, an internet service provider (ISP) that also launched a free email service the following August. (In 2001, Juno would merge with the ISP NetZero, after a prolonged patent battle, and became United Online.) The informal D. E. Shaw think tank also produced FarSight Financial, an online brokerage and internet-based personal financial services unit, later sold to Merrill Lynch.

But for Bezos, one idea in particular, born from freewheeling conversations between him and Shaw, caught his attention above all others. They called it the 'everything store'.

CHAPTER 2
START-UP

A little technological history is useful to frame Bezos' first steps into developing the Amazon company. Before the 1980s, computers and electronic networks were clunky, specialist affairs. Electronic computers were born in the 1950s, mainly in the arena of defence intelligence and command-and-control systems, especially in the context of nuclear weapon systems and forces. A challenge soon arose for those early computer engineers. It was quickly realized that it would be advantageous to develop systems that enabled the computers and the operators to 'talk' to one another over distance, thereby saving the time of operators physically moving between machines, while also avoiding the fiery risk of a single nuclear strike taking out the most important computer control system and leaving others helpless. Some progress was made in enabling computers to share a mainframe through separate terminals, but the really big leap forward came in 1965. In that year, Lawrence Roberts, a computer scientist at the MIT Lincoln Laboratory, demonstrated how two computers could communicate through an acoustic modem and telephone, sending the data down the line using 'packets', individual portions of data that chopped up larger messages into manageable chunks, reassembling them at the recipient's end to form a complete message. In 1967, Roberts moved to the US government's Advanced Research Projects Agency (ARPA), specifically the Information Processing Techniques Office (IPTO), where he worked on a new 'packet-switching' network called ARPANET (Advanced Research Projects Agency Network), striving to build an internationally capable digital communication network. Another great mind behind packet-switching and ARPANET was University of California, Los Angeles (UCLA) professor Leonard Kleinrock. On 29 October 1969, Kleinrock supervised a UCLA student, Charley Kline, in ARPANET's first message transmission, from a terminal in UCLA to another 645 km (400 miles) away in Stanford. This was, in essence, the birth of what we today call the internet.

ARPANET grew – by 1973, some 30 institutions across the world were able to talk electronically with each other across it, sending the early forms of email and various other data packages. But it was still the preserve of the academic and defence elite, well beyond the hands of the wider public. Several technological and commercial shifts changed this situation profoundly, as innovation began to sprint. In 1971, in Cambridge, Massachusetts, computer scientist Raymond Tomlinson developed the efficient email address format we know and love today, using the '@' sign to separate the name of the user from the computer destination. Various File Transfer Protocol (FTP) systems were engineered, making file sharing simpler. In 1974–8, US computer scientists Bob Kahn and Vint Cerf developed the Transmission Control Protocol/Internet Protocol (TCP/IP), which enabled computers to speak to one another in a common language and also for every computer to be given a unique IP address. In 1983, Paul Mockapetris and Jon Postel at the University of Southern California invented the Domain Name System, which could convert IP addresses (long strings of unmemorable numbers) into simple names. Crucially, the world's first personal computers (PCs) began to make their way into homes and offices during the 1970s, but in the 1980s they became cheap enough to reach a mass market. Computing was becoming a universal opportunity, and the world would never be the same again.

All these changes drove the growth of the computer network – known as the 'internet' (a term coined by Cerf and Kahn back in 1974) – so that by 1987 there were 30,000 hosts (devices capable of accessing the network) using it. But access to the interet was still largely confined to tech specialists. Then, in the late 1980s and early 1990s, British computer scientist Tim Berners-Lee, while working for the CERN (Conseil Européen pour la Recherche Nucléaire) particle-research laboratory in Geneva, Switzerland, essentially cracked open the internet for mass society. He developed HyperText Markup Language (HTML), opaque to outsiders but revolutionary in consequence. Pages of information written in HTML could be accessed over the internet using HyperText Transfer Protocol (HTTP), the individual document accessed through 'hyperlinks' that went to addresses in a Uniform Resource Identifier (URI) system; from the latter came the Uniform Resource Locator (URL) web addresses with which we are familiar. Most crucially, in 1990, Berners-Lee also produced a piece of 'browser' software designed so that anyone could access and read an HTML document. He called it the 'WorldWideWeb', and it became one of the seminal technological revolutions in human history. Now, effectively, the internet could be opened for business. Not coincidentally, ARPANET was formally decommissioned in 1990, as the internet expanded inexorably out into the private sector.

Browser capability improved significantly with the invention of the Mosaic software by US computer science student Marc Andreessen in 1993. It offered smooth functionality and elements that we now take for granted, such as the ability to install one piece of software on multiple operating systems and point-and-click internet access. A year later, Andreessen would rebrand his company, Mosaic Communications, into Netscape Communications with entrepreneur Jim Clark. From this move emerged Netscape Navigator, the powerhouse web browser of the mid-1990s, with 10 million users and 86 per cent market share in 1996. It worked perfectly on the new Microsoft Windows operating system, Windows 95, an interface that arrived in 1995 and was far more attuned to the rising internet age. Windows really showed society how useful computers could be. Note also that 1995 was the year in which Microsoft introduced its Internet Explorer browser as part of its Windows systems; by 1999, this browser would have more than reversed the market share figures with Navigator.

Regardless, the rush to the internet meant that by 1996 there were more than 100,000 websites in operation. The first e-commerce sites also made themselves known. Tellingly for our story here, Amazon was not the first online book retailer. That honour goes to Book Stacks Unlimited in Cleveland, developed by Charles M. Stack. Its searchable and catalogued Books.com website opened in 1994 and offered half a million titles, which eventually pulled in the same number of customers each month, who were able to pay for the products online via credit card. It drove sales through staff reviews and recommendations. Soon, there were a handful of similar online book stores dotted across the United States, and Bezos would have been aware of all of them. In fact, it was partly his dissatisfaction with the service offered by such stores that led him to see a gap in the market and believe he could do things better. The potential for growth in internet retail was formidable and Bezos knew it. Prior to starting Amazon, he calculated that internet traffic had increased by 230,000 per cent in just a year, and that this was just the beginning. If he was going to act, it had to be now. (As a slight corrective to our perception that online retail quickly became dominant, however, by 2010 online shopping still constituted only 6 per cent of all retail sales in the United States.)

THE BIRTH OF THE 'EVERYTHING STORE'

Bezos would sow his visions of a new online shopping experience in the fertile but risky soils of the early internet revolution. His own research data gave him a clear message: internet web traffic was seeing truly explosive growth, and this was just early days. His discussions with Shaw had convinced him of the viability of what they called the 'everything store', an online retailer that connected the ever-widening sea of internet customers with the rivers of manufacturers and vendors, all via an online retail interface and fast distribution network. But while Shaw saw this as an interesting discussion (although it would flower into a concrete investment later), Bezos felt a genuine calling. It was time to go it alone.

It was undoubtedly a challenging prospect to leave DESCO, a job that had given Bezos a creative working atmosphere, secure employment and an excellent income stream, to pursue a vision of online retailing. But as Bezos later explained in a presentation to the Commonwealth Club of California in 1998:

'I knew when I was eighty that I would never, for example, think about why I walked away from my 1994 Wall Street bonus right in the middle of the year at the worst possible time. That kind of thing just isn't something you worry about when you're eighty years old. At the same time, I knew that I might sincerely regret not having participated in this thing called the Internet that I thought was going to be a revolutionizing event. When I thought about it that way … it was an incredibly easy decision to make' (quoted in Stone 2018: 41).

Bezos would define this formula for making decisions about the future as the 'Regret Minimization Framework', and it is a crucial component of his entrepreneurial drive and risk-taking. Bezos has repeated and refined this formula over the years. In an interview with Mathias Döpfner for *Business Insider* in April 2018, Bezos explained that when it comes to their careers, people tend to regret the things they didn't do more than the things they did do, thus it is better to act in a way that minimizes the risk of future regret. Once he had done this in the case of the 'everything store', the decision was clear – he would have to leave DESCO, regardless (or perhaps because of) the risks.

Thus in late 1993, Bezos walked out of the doors of D. E. Shaw and began to climb the steep slopes of an internet start-up. A key question, though, was 'What will I sell?' Although the 'everything store' concept looked to the horizons of being a near universal seller of consumer goods, that wasn't going to be viable in the first instance. So Bezos decided that he would begin with one product category only – books.

In many ways, books were an ideal online retail product. The existing back catalogue of books was vast and accessible and in-print books were readily sourced through the two great book distributors operating at that time, Ingram and Baker & Taylor. The public appetite for reading was voracious, but it would also be practical to build up focused profiles of each customer's reading preferences, forming a powerful database to drive future sales. Regarding the practicalities of delivery, books were convenient – a product produced in mostly predictable sizes and formats with a regular, easily packaged shape, meaning that they would be convenient to pack and mail.

The product was chosen, but challenges abounded. The world of e-commerce was still very much in its infancy. This meant that almost every aspect of the interface and infrastructure would have to be worked up from scratch, all while overheads were ticking away and draining slim resources. Far more threatening were the monstrous competitors the plucky start-up would be running against, in the form of the major bookstore chains. By 1993, for example, Crown Books had 196 stores across the United States. Even greater in size and reach was Borders, which during the 1990s not only held a great swathe of the US book market, but also had a major international presence, its book superstores being as much destinations to eat, drink and socialize as they were to find and buy books. But the real leviathan of the book industry was Barnes & Noble (B&N). Particularly following its purchase of 797 B. Dalton bookstores in 1987, B&N was ruthless in its growth model. To give an idea of the scale of B&N compared to Amazon, when B&N launched its own online bookstore in 1997 (an event discussed in the following pages), Amazon had 125 employees and $60 million annual sales, whereas B&N had 30,000 employees and $3 billion in sales. There was a real danger, and one pointed out to Bezos by several potential investors, that as soon as Amazon popped its head above the parapet, B&N in particular would set up a rival service and use its immense capital and customer reach to crush Amazon before it could gather momentum.

All these factors taken into account, Bezos kept a zealous grip on his vision, believing that he could put himself at the forefront of internet innovation and stay ahead of his competitors, even the big ones, as they struggled to catch up. He was not blasé about the risks, however. Up front, he told many of the early investors in Amazon that there was a 70 per cent chance of failure. Some might have seen even those negative odds as being a bit too generous.

Relocation was required to give the fledgling business the right start, and Bezos chose Seattle in Washington State as his preferred destination. There was a strict calculus behind the decision. US commercial law stated that companies only had to pay sales tax in the state in which the company was located, thus it was sound thinking for companies to establish themselves in states with comparatively low populations, rather than those in which there would be many millions of customers (New York, for example). Seattle also had two other virtues – it was near an Ingram distribution warehouse, plus it was something of a destination for tech-heads, meaning that Bezos could tap into rich and relevant seams of expertise.

So, the first order of business was for Bezos and MacKenzie to move to Seattle. This was accomplished on a now-famous road trip in July 1994, during which the couple flew to Texas, borrowed Bezos' father's 1988 Chevy Blazer, then drove across the United States to Seattle. On the journey, Bezos tapped away at the keys of his laptop computer (evidently many of the roads were straight and flat), working out sales projections in an Excel sheet. In Seattle itself, Bezos' first business premises was the garage of his new home. Everything was on a shoestring. Bezos was starting the business with $10,000 of his own cash, supplemented by $84,000 in loans over the next six months (Stone 2018: 48), which was not a lot to finance a major tech start-up. In the garage, they set up tables from Home Depot – these would be the packing area – and they had to buy computers; this was an online company, after all.

Note that the name Bezos chose for his new venture was … Cadabra Inc. Although kind-of catchy, the title had a problem that was soon pointed out to Bezos – on the phone, the word 'Cadabra' often came across as the word 'cadaver', an image that did nothing for positive brand-building. There was a hunt, therefore, for a new name, and out of the whirlpool of possibilities Bezos conceived of Amazon. Naming the company after the great South American river, the largest on the planet, gave a sense not only of scale and ambition but also of flow and connection. The name stuck, and remains to this day as one of the most recognizable brands on the planet.

There was also the need to hire the company's first recruits. Bezos himself, although possessing a high level of tech knowledge and an unchallenged capacity for work, needed talented people to drive the company forward quickly. MacKenzie was the first employee, working on accounts, finance and administration, and helping Bezos assess people during hiring cycles. The first external recruit was Shel Kaphan. Kaphan had an academic background in mathematics and computer science, and since graduating from the University of California, Santa Cruz, had proficiently handled a variety of tech-centred jobs, including working for Kaleida Labs (a failed joint IBM and Apple venture to develop a cross-platform multimedia player) and the *Whole Earth Catalog* counterculture magazine, where he gained a strong hands-on insight into the mail-order business. Personal connections put him in contact with Bezos, and they met up to discuss the opportunities within the start-up. Kaphan later said that he was particularly impressed with Bezos as an individual, who struck him as hyper focused, sharply intelligent, driven to succeed, but also with a decent sense of humour – something they would need over the following months. Bezos was impressed with Kaphan in return, and hired him as vice president of Research & Development (R&D). Another early hire was Paul Davis, a British software developer who had emigrated to the United States in 1989. Davis worked in the Computer Science and Engineering Department at the University of Washington before taking posts in several software development companies. It would be Davis and Kaphan who were tasked with building the Amazon website.

Together, this small core team, in basic surroundings, would be responsible for laying the cornerstone that, unknown to them, would grow into one of the largest retail entities ever. On 1 November 1994, the Amazon URL was registered. The company now had to open for business. There was much to do, physically, financially and technologically. It soon became clear that having the Amazon distribution centre in the Bezos family garage simply wasn't going to work, so the nascent company moved to a small office plus an 18.5 sq m (200 sq ft) warehouse in the SoDo neighbourhood, part of Seattle's Industrial District. A sidenote – we should observe that during the epic journey to establish and grow Amazon, Bezos and MacKenzie also added the complexity of making a family. In total, they would have three sons and adopt a daughter. Clearly, life was going to be busy.

THE GROWTH YEARS

Jumping ahead momentarily in our chronology, in 1999, Jeff Bezos wrote one of his annual letters to shareholders. In it,

Bezos provided his shareholders with an insight into the state of the company as Amazon looked towards the impending sunrise of a new millennium. Reminding ourselves that the start-up had established itself just six years earlier (by which time, statistically, the majority of new companies will have failed), some of the basic stats Bezos offered were eye-catching: sales of $1.64 billion, which was an increase of 169 per cent over the previous year, with 90 per cent revenue growth in just three months; 16.9 million customers, up from 6.2 million at the beginning of the year; more than 73 per cent of orders placed by repeat customers; 22 per cent of sales outside the United States (principally the United Kingdom and Germany); a growth in physical distribution space from 27,870 sq m (300,000 sq ft) to more than 464,000 sq m (5 million sq ft) in less than 12 months.

Factoring in Bezos' own prediction that the company had a 70 per cent chance of failure when it started, how did Amazon get from a skeleton staff and an anonymous warehouse in Seattle to this thriving enterprise, which was still a shadow of the giant that it would go on to become? While we can factor in external market forces and the underestimated power of sheer luck, it is doubtless the case that the traction was truly generated by Bezos' relentless desire to push the company to higher and higher summits. The motto that prevailed in Amazon in its early days – 'Get Big Fast' – was a mantra for both survival and success.

With their URL registered, Amazon now had the more laborious challenge of producing a fully functioning e-commerce site. This was the 1990s, and still the formative days of computer programming, so nearly everything had to be coded from scratch, Bezos' programmers relying on the C computer programming language to develop the customer interface and the Berkeley DB system (itself created in C) to provide the database backend. The website was first tested on amenable family and friends. Famously, the first ever order on Amazon.com was made by one John Wainwright, a former colleague of Kaphan, on 3 April 1995, the purchased publication being *Fluid Concepts And Creative Analogies: Computer Models of the Fundamental Mechanisms Of Thought* by Douglas Hofstadter. In a posting on Quora (a social question-and-answer website) in 2013, Wainwright said that this purchase has remained in his order history and that he still had the packing slip and book. The initial website was wildly rudimentary compared to what many of us use today. It had a book search function (indexed through a major book distributor's catalogue), a shopping basket, and a checkout through which customers could make payment via their credit card. One innovation was the option for the customer to leave a book review. What was interesting about this was that the customer could leave *any* sort of review, including a negative one. To some, this was questionable – customers could actively undermine Amazon's efforts to sell titles – but Bezos insisted that the website serve the customers, not publishers or authors. If the customer placed an order, Amazon would acquire the publication from one of the book distributors, then package it and move it out. There was little profit margin on each sale, once the external players in the process had taken their cut.

The Amazon.com website finally went live to the public on 16 July 1995. Orders went from a trickle to a steady stream in a matter of days, with $14,000 of orders in Week 2. (At first, the Amazon staff would ring a bell when an order came in – that celebratory practice soon stopped.) Orders began to hit at a quicker pace

Jeff Bezos holds Amazon's first sign, spray painted for an interview with a Japanese TV station (1995).

once the new bookseller was featured on Yahoo, then one of the world's biggest search engines. It quickly became clear that the acceleration in sales was threatening to outstrip every aspect of the physical operation, from the customer database to the packing and distribution facilities, with the warehouse staff working at an unsustainable pace to fulfil orders. Amazon, as Bezos planned, needed to grow, and for that he required money. A lot more money.

Bezos set his sights on raising $1 million of funding, and he drew up a shortlist of investors. He worked the list himself, indefatigably travelling around the United States and using all his personal presence to convince each investor to sink money into this tech prospect. Many of the investors shied away, not least because most couldn't really understand the proposition in the first place; Bezos later said that the first question from most of the investors was 'What's the internet?' But in the end, 60 meetings later, Bezos had persuaded 22 people each to part with approximately $50,000, most of the investors convinced mainly by the irresistible confidence, character and intelligence of the man in front of them. Bezos had his money.

He put it to good use, with Amazon growing by 30 per cent by early 1996 (Stone 2018: 64). But under the 'Get Big Fast' standard, growth simply begat the need for more capital to fuel the future. Amazon was scaling up fast as its name and service began to spread – by March 1997, the website was averaging 80,000 hits per day. A major injection of cash came in 1995 with an $8 million investment from the venture capital firm Kleiner Perkins Caufield & Byers. (They made a good call – by 1999, they had returns of more than 55,000 per cent on their investment.) The further expansion made possible by this money meant that Bezos and his financial team, particularly the formidable Joy Covey as chief financial officer, began to prepare for an initial public offering (IPO, when a company first sells shares to the public). The underwriter for the IPO was Deutsche Bank and the process of defining the share value took a tortuous two months. For although Amazon was growing rapidly, there was still much uncertainty about whether it had a long-term future. Most significantly, Barnes & Noble were starting to take note of Amazon's upstart presence. Indeed, the Riggio brothers (Len and Steve) – tough characters who ran the B&N empire – arranged a meeting with Bezos, accompanied by Amazon board member Tom Alberg, in a Seattle restaurant. The B&N brothers politely but forcefully stated that B&N's upcoming online bookstore would crush Amazon, but that B&N could see areas in which they could work with Bezos' company. Some highly regarded analysts at this time were confidently predicting the destruction of Amazon along just these lines, but Bezos resisted the offers on the table. Ultimately, he believed that a small, fast and innovative company could outpace the slower-moving giants. He was right.

CHAPTER 3

THE BIG TIME

The Amazon IPO came out on 15 May 1997, each share at a price of $18 – not spectacular but still big enough to raise $54 million of capital to power Amazon operations onwards. We should note, however, that the meteoric growth in Amazon sales and the injections of capital didn't yet mean that it was making a profit. Far from it, in fact. In 1996, for example, Amazon revenues grew from $511,000 to $15.75 million, but its losses lay heavy on the other end of the see-saw, from $303,000 to $5.78 million. As soon as money appeared on the book Bezos ploughed it back into the company – growth was key at this stage, not profit.

LOOKING EVER AHEAD

An invaluable insight into Bezos' management approach and strategic philosophy comes from the various letters to shareholders that Bezos wrote annually. The one from 1997 has attained something of a legendary status, because in so many ways it still serves as a blueprint not only for the growth of the Bezos empire, but also for any ambitious start-up reaching for the commercial stars. After the letter's initial paragraphs outlining core growth figures and explaining that this was 'Day 1' of the internet, with all the opportunities that presented, Bezos explained that his focus was squarely on the horizon, not the ground immediately beneath his feet:

It's All About the Long Term

We believe that a fundamental measure of our success will be the shareholder value we create over the long term. This value will be a direct result of our ability to extend and solidify our current market leadership position. The stronger our market leadership, the more powerful our economic model. Market leadership can translate directly to higher revenue, higher profitability, greater capital velocity, and correspondingly stronger returns on invested capital.

Our decisions have consistently reflected this focus. We first measure ourselves in terms of the metrics most indicative of our market leadership: customer and revenue growth, the degree to which our customers continue to purchase from us on a repeat basis, and the strength of our brand. We have invested and will continue to invest aggressively to expand and leverage our customer base, brand, and infrastructure as we move to establish an enduring franchise.

In some ways this is a classic statement of the dotcom bubble era, in which there seemed limitless possibilities for growth in the sunlit uplands of direct digital access to customers. It was partly this viewpoint that led to the market's tolerance for gross overvaluations of many internet companies; losses didn't matter, it was ambition that counted. But note here how frequently the word 'customer' appears in Bezos' model. One of the subheadings further down the letter was 'Obsess Over Customers'. This absolute customer focus, and unrelenting desire to match the service with the optimal customer experience, was and remains the structural steelwork around which Amazon has been built. In some key business meetings Bezos would later have with potential partners and investors, he would somewhat theatrically leave a chair around the table empty – this was the customer's chair, and served to remind those present that whatever decisions were made between powerful individuals, ultimately those decisions had to orientate to customer value.

Further on in the letter, Bezos explained that 'Because of our emphasis on the long term, we may make decisions and weigh tradeoffs differently than some companies.' He clarified this point in a long series of bullet points, which included elements such as:

- '. . . investment decisions in light of long-term market leadership considerations rather than short-term profitability'
- 'We will make bold rather than timid investment decisions where we see a sufficient probability of gaining market leadership advantages'
- '. . . we choose to prioritize growth because we believe that scale is central to achieving the potential of our business model'
- 'We will continue to focus on hiring and retaining versatile and talented employees, and continue to weight their compensation to stock options rather than cash'

As we shall see, the overriding focus on long-term growth was subsequently modified to deal with the realities of cash flow and survival once the dot com bubble burst in the early 2000s. But the fusion of unwavering long-term expansion and a constant return to customer focus, to which we then add the relentless drive of Bezos and his teams, were together the engine that drove Amazon to succeed at unimaginable scale and to survive when so many other companies went to the wall or were gobbled up by others.

Amazon's IPO was just the beginning of an extraordinary effort in capital raising over the next three years, driven by the conviction Bezos and his company managed to instil in investors, plus the ambient fever pitch of enthusiasm for dot com stocks. Between 1998 and 2000, bond sales and other efforts raised a massive $2.2 billion for Amazon. Bezos diverted the money straight back into the business, adding key ingredients to the growth recipe – people (talent and general workers); distribution facilities; new innovations and additional income streams and services; acquisitions of other companies.

The first of those elements, the attraction and recruitment of new personnel, opens another window on Bezos' management perspective. Bezos values executive employees who are super-bright, highly driven to succeed, but who also offer a spectrum of skills and knowledge sometimes outside those traditionally valued in industry at senior levels. Thus a scientist or mathematician – a person who could see things from a new, highly insightful vantage point – might be appointed to a position more typically occupied by a project manager or someone with prior experience in the field. Bezos wants disrupters, not conformists. In an interview with the Reagan National Defense Forum (RNDF) in 2017, Bezos also outlined three characteristics for the ideal Amazon employee and the conditions in which those people work. Centrally, Bezos explained that he wants 'missionaries' not 'mercenaries'. He clarified by explaining that the missionary thrives on the ideal of success, not on executive perks: 'Missionaries care about the mission. It's actually not very complicated. And you can confuse people with free massages. Like, "Oh, I don't really like the mission here, but I love the free massages."' As we shall see, wire-tight frugality in operational management is another Bezos'principle, and there is doubtless an element of that at play here. But at the same time Bezos wants people driven by core values and a compulsive need to excel in achieving goals; a clock-watching preoccupation with getting to the next business perk is unlikely to be evidence of this personality trait. Furthermore, Bezos acknowledges that the business environment itself must support the expression of missionary zeal: 'But you can drive great people away—for example, by making the speed of decision-making really slow. Why would great people stay in an organization where they can't get things done? They look around after a while, and they're, like, "Look, I love the mission, but I can't get my job done because our speed of decision-making is too slow." So large companies like Amazon need to worry about that.'

The frenetic pace of life at Amazon's executive levels (actually, right down to the warehouse floor) is one area that has attracted controversy and comment over the years. It is certainly true that the personal Bezos pace can be matched and sustained by few, but here Bezos reframes the environment, seeing it as a space in which the ambitious can excel because there are few restrictions in their way. Later, Bezos would institute an award system in Amazon that would give credit to those who attempted to improve Amazon efficiency through self-starting innovation, even if the effort ultimately turned out to be unproductive. It seems to be the mindset Bezos pursues, as much as the skillset.

As Amazon's workforce steadily expanded to number in the hundreds, the ongoing recruitment drive became ravenous. At executive levels, the recruitment objectives were to bring people in who could demonstrate a clear potential contribution to the 'Get Big Fast' mantra. Notably, Amazon took significant numbers of senior executive from the vast US retailer Walmart, often with a view to acquiring Walmart's insight into economies of scale in product processing and distribution and strategies for handling customer and store information. New recruits included Rick Dalzell, a tough but popular former US Army Ranger and formerly vice president of the Information Systems Division at Walmart. He was headhunted repeatedly by Bezos and his team, and upon finally relenting, joined the company as chief information officer (CIO), focusing on the development of Amazon's computerized merchandising and distribution systems. Dalzell would spend ten years at Amazon, holding the position of senior vice president between 1997 and 2007 – the year he retired from the company. Another of the Walmart emigrants was Jimmy Wright, who had been the company's vice president of distribution. In total, Amazon took 15 of Walmart's current or former employees or consultants, and in 1998 this exodus even triggered Walmart to file a lawsuit against Amazon, claiming that it was attempting to steal Walmart trade secrets and also duplicate some of its processes. The action was eventually settled in 2002, largely in Amazon's favour; Walmart won nothing in damages and Amazon simply agreed to reassign one key person within the company and restrict the work assignments of eight others.

The Walmart personnel were just a handful of the many talented and driven individuals who stepped through Amazon's doors in the

There was some time for play amidst the hard work of building Amazon – here Jeff Bezos and early 'Amazonians' play broomball at a picnic in August 1999.

closing years of the 20th century. They ranged from people who had previously held high office in some of the largest corporations in the land down to young and hungry graduates, who brought little or no commercial experience but lots of youthful energy and ideas. The Amazon doors were revolving, however, and as many arrived, others left, burned out, failing to meet performance expectations or becoming sidelined by the influx of fresh, hungry executives. One of these was Shel Kaphan, who left in 1999, having played a foundational role in the creation of the Amazon legend.

Hiring the best talent was, and remains, at the core of Bezos' project model. To get the workforce buying into this aspiration, in 1999 Bezos introduced the 'Barkeeper Program'. Its initial focus was on the hiring of exceptional new tech personnel, and it involved bringing an objective third party into the interview process, a person with a developing track record of recruiting high-performing people. An implication of this process is that a person can improve their own status in the company by recruiting individuals who are better than both themselves and those around them. Indeed, the 'Bar Raiser Program', as it is currently called, states that 'Every person hired should be better than 50 per cent of those currently in similar roles.'

Amazon's full-afterburner growth required the expansion of facilities as well as people. One of the great migraines of Amazon's early years was ensuring that the company had the physical space and fulfilment systems to process the rising floodwater of orders. In 1999 alone, the company spent some $300 million on new distribution centres across the United States. These plants included high investment in automated order processing and packaging systems, but they remained very heavily dependent upon manpower. In some legendary pre-Christmas rush periods, even senior executives were sent to the warehouse floor in the push to ensure that every customer's order was met in time for Christmas Day, an effort that involved people sleeping in cars and offices, cancelling Christmas breaks with family, and working through multiple nights. As we have already noted, for Bezos, the customer sat at the apex of the Amazon hierarchy, not executive comfort.

The late 1990s was also a time in which Amazon began to make its next steps towards becoming the 'everything store', by branching out beyond books. Bezos realized that being a bookseller had limited horizons, a message reinforced by statistical and financial analysis from his team. It was also a more competitive landscape than even just a few years previously. Some of the threats were seen off or kept under control. B&N, for example, launched its online store, BarnesandNoble.com, in 1997, but it couldn't catch up with its nimbler rival, who would attract ever larger numbers of customers by branching out into product lines beyond the remit of the great bookseller. Other competing services caused Bezos and the Amazon team greater concern. In 1995, French-born technology entrepreneur Pierre Omidyar launched the online auction site eBay, which went through a growth trajectory every bit as steep as Amazon's – the site conducted 250,000 auctions in 1996, but

Amazon's growth quickly began to accelerate once the website went live in July 1995. Here Jeff Bezos holds aloft Amazon's millionth customer order in October 1997.

200,000 in January 1997 alone. By 2000, eBay had 12 million registered users. Bezos had reason to be unsettled. Here, in essence, was an alternative and genuine 'everything store' (in 2000, there were 4.5 million inventoried items for sale every day on eBay), albeit one conducted through individual auctions, which relieved the eBay business of the headache of warehousing and distribution.

eBay would remain a peer rival of Amazon for many years. In fact, in 1998, Bezos and Omidyar met personally, on Bezos' invitation, in Seattle. Several ideas were floated during these discussions, including Amazon having links to eBay when customers couldn't find specific items on the Amazon site, and the possibility that Bezos himself might be an investor in eBay. The discussions didn't reach practical output. Omidyar and his team felt their model for growing e-commerce was ultimately stronger

Taking his focus on customer service to its fullest extent, Jeff Bezos hand-delivers the millionth order to an Amazon customer in October 1997.

than that presented by Amazon, not least because eBay didn't have the huge infrastructural commitment of warehouses, stocking and distribution.

Sensing that eBay would become an undermining challenge to Amazon, Bezos attempted to take a slice of the online auction market by setting up an eBay rival, Amazon Auctions, in March 1999. In a CBS interview published on 8 April 1999, Bezos explained that 'I think there is room for lots of players. What we've tried to do is take our tradition of making things simple, as easy as possible, and move that into the auction space. We had one-click shopping, and now we have "bid click," which makes it easy to bid at auctions.' Just two weeks later, Amazon bought out online auction pioneer LiveBid, attempting to gain further traction in the sector. Both Amazon Auctions and LiveBid were destined for short-lived failure – a story to which we shall return.

The establishment of Amazon Auctions was just one indicator of Bezos' fidgety desire to expand Amazon's roots into far broader product marketplaces in the late 1990s – it was time to stop just being the world's most successful online bookseller. The focus of the expansion in 1998–9 was specifically music, DVDs, toys and electronics. The first two of these markets proved to be highly successful for Bezos and his team, the format of the products (easily postable CDs and DVDs) and the access to convenient distributors making for a relatively smooth addition to the Amazon product line. Toys and electronic goods were an entirely different matter. Here, the headache for Amazon was that it would have to deal directly with the manufacturers or key stockists, rather than major distributors. This meant interacting with big, aggressive players in the markets, the likes of Hasbro, Sony and Toshiba, who were naturally focused on driving the best deals for their companies, rather than the optimal opportunities for Amazon. The resulting supply problems meant that Amazon had to scramble around for stock, including using secondary distributors; there were even occasions around the 1999 Christmas season when Amazon executives essentially had to raid local branches of Toys "R" Us with their credit cards, frantically snapping up popular brands of toys to resell and ensure that Amazon customers received their goods in time for the holiday.

The move into toys and electronics illustrates the importance Bezos placed on thinking big. Much to the consternation of many of the leadership team around him, Bezos wanted to sink $120 million into toys alone (Stone 2018: 112), stocking a vast range of goods to satisfy every child's desire and parent's pocket, no matter how obscure. This alarmed Harrison Miller, the man appointed to head the new toys division. Notably, Miller had no experience in toys and little in retail but was hired more for his attitude and dynamism than closely matched experience. The toy market was notoriously hard to judge in terms of its trends, fashions and timings, and the 'think big' vision felt like an extraordinary risk. Furthermore, the way that the toys were sourced meant that once Amazon bought them it was stuck with them, raising the red-flag prospect of piled-high volumes of unsold stock. Indeed, this was exactly how it played out. After the 1999 holiday season, Amazon was left with $39 million of unsold toys that had to be written off. The fact that 1999 had seen overall Amazon sales rise an astonishing 95 per cent meant that the company was in a position to handle such a blow, but the scale of losses was mounting and Amazon had not yet turned a profit.

The late 1990s was a time in which Bezos lit additional burners under his ambition. As millions of dollars of sales and investment flowed into Amazon, Bezos embarked on a voracious programme of acquisitions, buying up companies that he felt would move Amazon further into positions of market dominance while also expanding the products and services Amazon could offer to a receptive public. Hundreds of millions went into buying companies such as IMDb, Bookpages, Telebuch, Exchange.com, PlanetAll, and Alexa Internet. (On 26 April 1999 alone, Amazon announced $645 million of stock transactions.) The companies Bezos bought also seemed to be surfing the wave of irresistible growth in the new online marketplace. Bookpages, for example, was the UK's largest online bookseller, with a choice of 1.2 million books and monthly growth figures of 28 per cent. Exchange. com was an online market specialist that operated two websites: www.bibliofind.com for hard-to-find or rare books (9 million listings) and www.musicfile.com (3 million listings) for specialist recordings and music memorabilia, sold through a network of small retailers, dealers and private collectors. Alexa Internet was a web traffic analysis company, which had insight and tools that enabled the better customization of web search and experience to customer needs – this company was acquired by Amazon for $250 million in stock. In 1998, for $170 million in Amazon stock, Bezos bought Junglee.com, a young and exciting online price comparison website.

Each of the new acquisitions seemed to lock in another piece of a vast but infinitely growing jigsaw. Alongside the takeovers and acquisitions, Bezos also invested heavily in companies he found exciting and that thoroughly diversified his portfolio, including

Gear.com, Pets.com, Wineshopper.com, Homegrocer.com and Greenlight.com (Stone 2018: 94).

The outrush of Amazon money and stock was also accompanied by Bezos' even loftier visions of what Amazon might became. Some of these were so gratuitously ambitious that they were labelled 'fever dreams' by Amazon executives, who were often truly alarmed by what the propositions would entail for a company already struggling to keep chaos at bay. There was the Alexandria Project, for example, for which Bezos wanted to stock two copies of every book ever printed in two of Amazon's US warehouses. Then there was Project Fargo – where the ambition was to stock one of *every product* ever manufactured. Defiant reality and pushback from Amazon executives meant that these vaulted visions never took off. They do, however, illustrate recurrent points about the Bezos mindset. The first is that the customer had to take absolute priority, regardless of the cost – both Alexandria and Fargo were examples of Bezos attempting to guarantee that all customers could always get exactly what they wanted. Second, it shows how Bezos has always oriented to maximum scale in his thinking – even if the intended project doesn't reach fulfilment, something will certainly happen.

THE BUBBLE BURSTS

By 1999, America and the world had fully noticed Jeff Bezos. That year he was named *Time* magazine's Man of the Year, a choice justified by the magazine's editor because 'Bezos is a person who not only changed the way we do things but helped pave the way for the future.' Bezos described the announcement as 'an incredible and humbling honour'. And yet, troubled times were stirring and darkening the clouds on the horizon, not only for Amazon but for the entire community of online commerce.

At the beginning of the 2000s, many financial analysts began to question the sustainability and scale of the dotcom bubble. Increasing instances of failed dotcom companies raised the possibility that inexhaustible e-commerce growth was actually something of a mirage, one that couldn't transcend the simple gravity of profit and loss. Amazon, as phenomenal as its growth had been, was also now a target of scepticism in some quarters. After all, despite having hit $8 billion worth of sales in 1998, Amazon still had yet to turn a profit. It was experiencing heightened levels of chaos, with its warehouses, stocking, distribution and data management all stretched to and beyond their outer limits by the roaring growth in sales. Some analysts predicted that Amazon was destined for a brutal arrest to its growth, and even possible collapse. The share price began to retreat, then plunged as the company went into the first year of the new millennium.

But Bezos was not a man to fold under pressure, as was captured in 2000 by his stark but defiant message to shareholders: 'Ouch. It's been a brutal year for many in the capital markets and certainly for Amazon.com shareholders. As of this writing, our shares are down more than 80 percent from when I wrote you last year. Nevertheless, by almost any measure, Amazon.com the company is in a stronger position now than at any time in its past.' The contrast between the precipitous slide in the value of Amazon stock and Bezos' ebullient emphasis on Amazon's resilience says much again about his way of looking at the world through the long-view lens. Later in the letter to shareholders, he takes the investor Benjamin Graham's statement that 'In the short term, the stock market is a voting machine; in the long term, it's a weighing machine,' and uses it to explain Amazon in its proper temporal context: 'We're a company that wants to be weighed, and over time, we will be – over the long term, all companies are. In the meantime, we have our heads down working to build a heavier and heavier company.' He extends his argument by explaining that the full shopping basket of acquisitions was part of the general 'land rush' for the internet. The overall impression here is of a man trying to build mass and seize territory, in much the same way that settlers spreading out into the American West in the 18th and 19th centuries tried to grab as much land as they could, without necessarily knowing what they were going to do with it.

Another apparent characteristic noted of Bezos by those who have known him is his indefatigable resilience in the face of problems, regardless of the scale. In fact, serious problems seem to produce one of two reactions, or both in sequence. Bezos is capable of explosive bursts of anger, especially in the face of incompetence or wilful ignorance – he needs his team to be absolutely on the ball with facts, figures and explanations, and woe betide the unprepared executive in one of his meetings. But he also seems to be one of those rare individuals who to a degree thrives on problems, treating them either as future victories once the challenges have been overcome or future opportunities only spotted in the process of combat. Either way, everything contributes to an ultimately upward direction, so long as the entrepreneur has the patience and confidence to endure.

But make no mistake, 1999 and 2000 were tough years for Bezos, and indeed the whole global economy, as the dotcom bubble finally burst in dramatic fashion. In March 2000, the respected financial magazine *Barron's* ran a cover headline that foretold: 'Burning Up; Warning: Internet companies are running out of cash—fast'. The NASDAQ Composite tech stock market index began a precipitous fall shortly after, and it would keep going down as numerous internet companies fulfilled *Barron's* prophecy – by October 2002, the NASDAQ-100 was down 78 per cent in comparison to its peak.

Amazon and Bezos were fully caught up in this decline, especially as it seemed to fulfil the pattern of a company that made no profit while shelling out hundreds of millions on investments. Many of Bezos' investments, acquisitions or innovations collapsed. Pets.com, in which Amazon had a 30 per cent stake, went out of business in November 2000, just nine months after its IPO. Bookpages, bought for $55 million, was wound up because, in essence, there was no point keeping it open in competition with Amazon. A Junglee-derived feature called 'Shop the Web' was quickly dropped as it was soon realized the Amazon didn't want customers leaving the Amazon.com website to go elsewhere (although Junglee did later help Amazon enter the India market). Amazon Auction stopped being promoted just a year after the service was developed and disappeared shortly after. On top of these and numerous other commercial dead-ends were the extreme costs of expanding warehouse and distribution facilities and the rising numbers of employees.

These problems were not distant ones for the wider Amazon staff, many of whom had been optimistic shareholders in their own company and saw the value of their personal investments plummet. For some, the consequences were even more severe – about 15 per cent of the Amazon workforce was laid off, including the 250 staff of an international call centre located in The Hague, Netherlands. Even more alarming, there was some market data seeming to indicate that the public's appetite for online shopping might be about to contract – the entire rationale of investing in dotcom stocks and services was possibly about to be undermined.

Amazon was teetering on the brink and Bezos was under a vice-like pressure, although those who saw him operate often noted an unflappable, upbeat character. Eventually Bezos was convinced, however, about the need for more stringent control of costs and a focus on moving towards the model of a profitable company. Significant changes were made during this period. The guiding Amazon mantra 'Get Big Fast' was replaced with the sensibly Victorian 'Get Our House in Order'. New managers were brought in with the aim of steering the company towards financial health. In 1999, one of the most significant appointments was a tough-as-nails executive called Joe Galli, formerly president of Worldwide Power Tools and Accessories at the Black & Decker power tools company. Galli's entrepreneurial mindset (his most famous quotation is 'Excuses are for other people') and operational discipline were seen as a balance to the more soaring visionary leadership offered by Bezos. Galli was appointed, with Bezos' consent, as president and chief executive officer (CEO), meaning that he was essentially in charge of the company. It was not to be a successful Amazon leadership model. Not only did Bezos, in practical terms, still retain a controlling hand over the direction of the company, but Galli's style of management clashed with many other executives', despite the fact that he was introducing some valuable changes to the company. Eventually, tensions built up to crisis point and in July 2000 Galli left the company, explaining that 'I'm just not a great number two', in reference to Bezos. Bezos was firmly at the helm again.

THE AMAZON FLYWHEEL

Given the depth of the crisis in the early 2000s, it is remarkable that Amazon survived. But more than that, it not only survived but would eventually emerge even more galvanized for future greatness. The key ingredient to the company's emergence on the other side of the burst bubble seems to be in large measure Bezos' iron grip on the principle of 'customer first', a focus all too easily lost when companies are struggling to keep their heads above the waterline. Often, such companies get caught in a death spiral, cutting costs and in the process degrading the customer experience, which leads to a further decline in sales, and so on. But Amazon kept innovating throughout, and thus as the new millennium progressed it would see accelerated growth to a scale that few could have predicted, except perhaps Bezos himself.

Some of the refinements implemented were seemingly subtle adjustments to the web experience, but which at scale had major impacts on sales. Back in June 1998, the Amazon Sales Rank (ASR) feature was introduced, which ranked the sales of all books and music, producing what was in effect a huge extension of a bestsellers list. ASR had two effects. The first was that customers could see how popular a particular title was in relation to other titles, and this influenced their sales behaviour; the more popular a book was in its sales rankings, the more popular it then became, in a virtuous circle of sales. Furthermore, authors, artists and publishers also bought into the competitive nature of the rankings and were thereby motivated to inject extra effort into publicity to squeeze the books up the ranks. (In time, of course, there would be accusations that some publishers were buying their own books from Amazon, and leaving highly positive reviews, to attain higher sales rankings.) A year later came another seminal technological improvement. In September 1999, the United States Patent and Trademark Office (USPTO) issued patent US 5960411 to Amazon. com for a feature called 'One-Click'. This system, developed by Amazon engineer Peri Hartman, meant that customers could store key payment and delivery information direct in their personalized Amazon account. When they wanted to purchase an item, they could click on the 'One-Click' or '1-Click' button for instant payment and fulfilment. It made the buying experience whip-crack quick, plus provided an on-screen bull's eye that was a gift for customers struggling to overcome their buying inhibitions or who were given to impulse buying. One-Click would be a resounding success, attested by the fact that B&N attempted to replicate it with an 'Express Lane' option on its own website, an effort quashed in the law courts when Amazon sued for patent infringement at the end of the year. (The case was finally settled in 2002.)

Other steps Bezos took to ensure the company remained customer focused were in relation to pricing. Bezos was a believer in deep discounting. One of the most high-profile demonstrations of this came in July 2000 when J.K. Rowling's *Harry Potter and the Goblet of Fire* was published. The novel was the fourth in the *Harry Potter* series and was awaited by millions of expectant readers in something akin to a literary feeding frenzy. Amazon plugged itself into the moment by offering readers an improbably generous 40 per cent discount on the cover price, to which it added express delivery for the same price as normal delivery, meaning that the readers who ordered in advance would receive the book on the very day it was published. To fulfil orders of the 1.2 kg (2.7 lb), 752-page book, Amazon enlisted the help of FedEx Home Delivery and FedEx Express to deliver the first 250,000 orders, an effort that involved 9,000 FedEx delivery personnel. By 12:01am on Saturday 8 July, a total of 350,020 copies of the book had been ordered from Amazon.com, and Bezos lost money on every copy. While that caused dismay among those eager for Amazon to reach profit, Bezos understood that providing this service would entrench the Amazon brand in the minds of hundreds of thousands of people who were thrilled to receive the book, and it would generate far wider publicity for the company.

A few months after the high-profile Harry Potter offer, a meeting took place with Amazon's 'S Team', a group of senior leaders within the company responsible for innovation and improvement. (Originally it had been called the J Team, but the name was later changed to S Team, the 'S' standing for 'Senior'. At the outset, the S Team consisted of the head of Tech, head of HR, head of Legal, head of Ops and head of Retail.) At this meeting, Bezos and his executives laid the foundation of a service that lit the touchpaper of dynamic growth at Amazon. It would be called Amazon Marketplace. The concept they developed was simple yet profoundly altered the business model. In Marketplace, third-party sellers could sell new or second-hand products directly alongside Amazon's own product lines, not siloed out in a separate area. Thus a customer searching for a particular product would see third-party options displayed alongside Amazon's inventory, and were presented with options about whom they wanted to buy from. Marketplace also gave Amazon the advantage that it collected a commission on every third-party sale, with the bonus that if it did not have the item in stock itself then the customer would still be able to purchase the item through Amazon. The same could not be said entirely of some of Amazon's executives, who felt that the pressure to clear inventories from Amazon warehouses was now compromised by the fact that customers could buy directly from external businesses.

But for Bezos, the critical point of Marketplace was that the customer was kept happy and would be even more wedded to Amazon as a single point for their online shopping. A crucial Bezos principle was at play here, borrowed and refined from a book by influential business consultant Jim Collins, *Good to Great*. This has been called the 'marketing flywheel', and it is central to grasping the rationale behind Bezos' extreme customer-facing outlook. In engineering, a flywheel is essentially a kind of mechanical battery, a heavy wheel mechanism rotating around an axis, storing kinetic energy as it gets faster and faster. The key point is that the flywheel is hard to get going from standstill, but the faster it goes, the more energy it builds up. Applying that principle to the world of Marketplace and e-commerce, the idea was that improvements to the customer experience result in an increase in customer traffic to the website. The increase in traffic attracts more and more third-party sellers, who naturally want to tap into the ever-expanding customer database. The increase in third-party sellers expands the product selection on the website, and the resulting competition produces lower prices for the customer. Lower prices mean an improved customer experience and the cycle begins again.

Marketplace attracted its fair share of negative scrutiny when it was launched, not least from book publishers, who feared that the sale of second-hand books online through Amazon's powerful interface would erode publisher profits and author royalties. But from Amazon's perspective, despite the internal resistance from some of its executives, the new service quickly proved its worth. Within four months of its launch, Marketplace sales grew by 200 per cent, with 250,000 customers having made at least one purchase from the service. In a press release in March 2001, Bezos would state that:

> The Amazon Marketplace success is driven by one thing and one thing alone – it creates real value for customers. There's always been a huge desire among customers to buy used, rare and collectible merchandise, and we're only beginning to understand how Amazon Marketplace can channel that demand to benefit customers, manufacturers, publishers, artists and the industry as a whole. We're confident that this model will continue to evolve, and believe it has the potential to drive meaningful category growth over the long term.

Taking the last sentence here, he was absolutely right. Looking into the future, in 2016, some 10,000 sellers operating in Marketplace generated a total of more than $1 billion in online sales. The rush to get on to the site absolutely confirmed the flywheel principle – more than 1,029,528 new sellers joined in 2017 alone, and today the figure rests north of 2 million. We should also acknowledge that Bezos found another advantage in bringing the outside world of sellers into the Amazon platform – Amazon could build up data profiles from third-party sales, monitoring which products sold particularly well and where demand seemed to be increasing.

This meant that Amazon's competitors laid bare their sales and marketing data for Amazon to exploit, and often a high-selling third-party product line would appear in Amazon's own inventory within months of the seller joining Marketplace. For Bezos, nothing mattered except the moment of encounter between the customer and Amazon.

Another Amazon innovation in the early years of the 2000s also added to the escape velocity required to defy the bursting of the dotcom bubble. In spring 2001, Bezos had an inspirational meeting with Jim Sinegal, the co-founder and former CEO of Costco, one of the great American retail success stories. During the meeting, Sinegal explained to the attentive entrepreneur how Costco set its pricing model, especially its focus on marketing, through customer expectations of rock-bottom prices. Bezos took this principle back to his S Team and the decision was made to make Amazon the go-to site for low prices, products being cheaper than customers could get them elsewhere (the Amazon pricing algorithms would be changed to track and match/beat prices offered by rival sellers). In books, music and videos alone this resulted in a 20–30 per cent price drop in July 2001 (Stone 2018: 160).

The drop in prices was an unnerving blow to some Amazon executives looking to attain profitability. But cumulatively, the improvements in customer experience started to show evidence as Amazon turned its first profit, albeit a tiny one (1 cent per share), in the fourth quarter of 2001. It was a clear sign that Amazon was not going to fulfil the prophecies of some financial doomsayers. What's more, Amazon had only laid down its roots in 1994, and now it was one of the world's biggest online retailers. Bezos had steered the company to this position through his unswerving focus on the customer and his relentless appetite for innovation, improvement and expansion. It is notable that even among the many failed investments and acquisitions of this time, Bezos often managed to pick up something valuable as he climbed up off the floor. The idea of the Alexandria Project, for example, would feed into the development of e-books and the Amazon Kindle (covered in the next chapter). Through the Junglee venture, Bezos had the fortuitous opportunity to meet two young and ambitious PhD students – Larry Page and Sergey Brin – who in 1998 launched a new web search service, called Google. Bezos was impressed by the venture and invested $250,000 in the start-up, at 4 cents a share. The evolution of Bezos' investment is unclear, but at Google's IPO in 2004 it was reported that Bezos held 3.3 million shares. Interestingly, press reporting in 2009 said that Bezos no longer held Google stock, at a time when it would have been worth $1.9 billion. But as we shall see in the next chapter, Google's rise showed that Amazon could by no means adopt a complacent position as it went deeper into the new millennium.

CHAPTER 4
THE GROWTH MODEL

In the early 2000s, Amazon was a triumph of growth and innovation. But its future greatness was still not a done deal. Amazon had certainly survived the dotcom crisis, but mere survival and stasis are not part of Bezos' model – he was still focused upon rolling, exponential growth. With growth, however, came costs as well as opportunities. The seminal challenge for Bezos and Amazon was ensuring that efficiency was able to keep pace with expansion. In many ways, the company that Bezos had created was, at the beginning of the 2000s, a sprawling and in many places rather chaotic organization, one that had evolved piecemeal in processes and product lines, with various imperfect sticking plasters and localized adaptations keeping the company running. For Amazon to keep growing, the underlying fault lines had to be identified, managed and eventually eliminated.

INTERNAL REFORMS

This book, with its primary focus on the life and achievements of Bezos himself, inevitably somewhat skirts over the many, many individuals who were integral to the realization of his dreams. But some need particular mention, and one such is Jeff Wilke. Wilke was another Princeton man, having gained a BSE degree in chemical engineering (*summa cum laude*) in 1989, after which he spent years working in a variety of demanding operational and management roles in polymer, chemical and electronics industries, up to boardroom level. In 1999, Wilke was vice president and general manager at AlliedSignal, but was approached by Amazon recruiter Scott Pitasky, who tried, and succeeded, in tempting Wilke over to Amazon.

Wilke's new remit was to oversee the transformation of Amazon's currently strained logistics and distribution infrastructure. Wilke was very much cut from the same cloth as Bezos. An innovator by nature, he hired a new team to handle the work – like Bezos, he didn't go down the familiar route of recruiting all industry logisticians, but also brought on board scientists, mathematicians and coders. Together, Wilke and his team set about completely reworking the logistical systems.

The new company mantra was 'Get Our House In Order', the focus being on improving efficiency in process and management. At one point, Wilke closed a struggling fulfilment centre (FC) at McDonough, its 450 staff becoming redundant; Wilke explained to Stone that it had been hard to get the right leaders or enough people to work at the fulfilment centre (Stone 2018: 209). At the same time, there was some streamlining of the executive levels of the company, striving to make the company leaner and more intrinsically innovative. Those most at risk of losing their positions were a) anyone deemed to be underperforming or lacking commitment (i.e. not demonstrating the ability to work around the clock); and b) generic project managers without interesting technical skills. As part of his efficiency journey, Bezos made personal visits to FCs, where he examined the plants, making hands-on investigations of every corner, machine, process and idea that underpinned his company. Anything or anyone that caught his attention or flagged his curiosity would be rigorously questioned, and subsequent improvements made to process or personnel.

Wilke and Bezos worked well together, and steadily the reformist efforts began to bear fruit. One of the key problems they tackled was reducing downtime in the fulfilment process. A particularly nagging issue was the method of working in 'batches'. When orders came into an FC, they would be distributed to staff 'pickers' who, in synchronized 'waves', were sent out around the warehouse to find and select the items. The picked items would then be placed into carts referred to as 'totes', after which the totes would go on to conveyor belts that ran into a sorting machine, which in turn organized the products into the individual customer orders for subsequent packing and shipping. The problem was that everyone in the batch process had to finish collecting their items before the sorting process could kick into life, meaning that there was lots of downtime while waiting for the slowest person in the wave to complete the task. The whole process was a stop-and-start affair.

Bezos and Wilke and his team found the solution to the problem by completely re-engineering the algorithms that governed the fulfilment process, writing the code internally and thereby freeing Amazon from reliance upon third-party software systems. This striving for independence from external suppliers and providers is another hallmark of Bezos' management direction. Integration with a third party can be beneficial, but generally, Bezos does not like anything that begins to smack of restrictive dependency – freedom to manoeuvre and solve problems self-sufficiently has certainly enabled Amazon to achieve a greater tempo of innovation than many established and upcoming competitors. Some years later, in a 2012 letter to shareholders, Bezos captured something of the intellectual engine that to this day drives Amazon's continual desire to stay ahead of the game:

> One advantage – perhaps a somewhat subtle one – of a customer-driven focus is that it aids a certain type of proactivity. When we're at our best, we don't wait for external pressures. We are internally driven to improve our services, adding benefits and features, before we have to. We lower prices and increase value for customers before we have to. We invent before we have to. These investments are motivated by customer focus rather than by reaction to competition. We think this approach earns more trust with customers and drives rapid improvements in customer experience – importantly – even in those areas where we are already the leader.

Being a market leader is not a static trophy. For Bezos, being at the front of the pack is not a cause for complacency, but rather an invitation to innovate and invent more, creating a continual acceleration in customer focus.

The measures taken to bring about a leaner and more efficient Amazon were not without their accompanying controversies. Some 16 years after its launch, Amazon and Bezos already had reputations for pushing staff and processes extremely hard, while watching every penny of what might be deemed unnecessary expenditure. For example, senior Amazon executives were often not allowed to fly business class, contra the standard perk of executives in most other large corporates. (Bezos himself had started to use a private jet to fly to many of his meetings around the United States but reminded those who accompanied him that he personally was paying for the jet, not Amazon.) All Amazon managers were expected to work with zealous commitment, and Amazon's consumption of evenings and weekends meant that for many the notion of a 'work-life balance' was little but a heady dream.

Away from senior management, there was also restlessness amongst some seasonal warehouse workers. In the quest for optimal FC efficiency, the performance of the pickers and other manual staff was tracked meticulously by time and performance. A points system was developed to log employee infractions, and this is still in use today (at least at the time of writing). Employees are allocated points for each violation, such as being late, taking too many sick days or not showing up at all. If the employee reaches six points in a 90-day period, then the person may be fired, unless there are extenuating circumstances. Press stories claimed that the heavy monitoring of employees squeezed morale, which in some places was further depressed by poor environmental conditions – there were stories of staff passing out in superheated summertime FCs or working in arctic-type clothing in deep winter.

Bezos' relationship to his employees has certainly been one of the more publicly scrutinised aspects of his approach to management. Viewed from his absolute commitment to customer experience, many press accusations seem more sins of omission than sins of commission – Bezos has simply sought to optimize the system for the benefit of the customer, following that logic wherever it leads. But inevitably, Bezos had to face pushback, with discontent in some quarters (although it was far from universal) leading to sporadic

Amazon worker unionization drives from major US unions, the list of publicly expressed grievances including working conditions and pay. In 2000, the Communications Workers of America and the United Food and Commercial Workers made some of the first failed efforts to unionize Amazon workers, and in 2001, the Washington Alliance of Technology Workers claimed that 850 workers were specifically targeted for layoffs in Seattle after an effort at unionization there; Amazon flatly denied there was any connection between the two events.

There were further industrial disputes in the 2010s, including significant ones in Delaware in 2014 and Chester, Virginia, in 2016, but one of the biggest and bitterest was that at the FC in Bessemer, Alabama, in 2020. Here, the Retail, Wholesale and Department Store Union (RWDSU) filed with the National Labor Relations Board (NLRB) for a major unionization of FC workers. It led to an acrimonious and extended legal battle, with Amazon receiving repeated accusations of heavy-handed anti-union tactics. The pressure grip on Bezos and his company was squeezed tighter by wider political involvement, with several US Representatives and Senators siding with the overall thrust of the union cause; even the newly appointed President Joe Biden aligned himself with the workers' movement, as the case rolled on into 2021. Eventually, an employee ballot was held on 29 March 2021 and when the votes were counted a week later, the votes against unionization were overwhelming: 1,798 to 738. This did not entirely end the controversy, as a subsequent NLRB report concluded that 'a free and fair election was impossible', noting that it was a 'possibility that the employer's misconduct influenced some of these 2,000 eligible voters [who did not vote]'.

Although the Bessemer dispute was between Amazon and its workers, and not Bezos per se, the Amazon leader naturally came in for a lot of severe judgements from some corners of the press, who accused him of placing profit well above workers' rights and conditions. In a further letter to shareholders, however, Bezos showed a reflective awareness of the discussions:

Our relationship with employees is a very different example. We have processes they follow and standards they meet. We require training and various certifications. Employees have to show up at appointed times. Our interactions with employees are many, and they're fine-grained. It's not just about the pay and the benefits. It's about all the other detailed aspects of the relationship too.

Does your Chair take comfort in the outcome of the recent union vote in Bessemer? No, he doesn't. I think we need to do a better job for our employees. While the voting results were lopsided and our direct relationship with employees is strong, it's clear to me that we need a better vision for how we create value for employees – a vision for their success.

If you read some of the news reports, you might think we have no care for employees. In those reports, our employees are sometimes accused of being desperate souls and treated as robots. That's not accurate. They're sophisticated and thoughtful people who have options for where to work. When we survey fulfillment center employees, 94% say they would recommend Amazon to a friend as a place to work.

It is clear from the tone of this piece that Bezos is stung by the accusations, and keen to give a counterbalance to the narrative that Amazon was a callous employer. In other documents, Amazon pointed to figures such as lower-than-usual industrial injury rates among employees, to show that it was not dismissive of working conditions. But what was also clear was that Bezos' growth model was creating tens of thousands of jobs around the United States and abroad, often in places where they were much needed.

PRIME IDEAS

Even as the ripples from the burst tech bubble began to subside, Bezos was tilting the nose cone of Amazon once more in an upward direction, with a new wave of innovations and expansions. As Amazon grew, it also acquired more muscle for buying and negotiation, which created a virtuous circle of cost savings and profits that would massively transform the trading accounts of the company. For example, in 2002 Amazon decided to renegotiate the shipping rates with its biggest delivery supplier, United Parcel Service (UPS). At the time, UPS had an unrivalled reach in the United States, and thus it rejected Amazon's requests for discounted rates, believing that Amazon had no scalable option but to stick with UPS at the fixed prices. Amazon promptly threatened UPS that if they didn't discount their rate, Amazon would take its millions of packages to Federal Express (FedEx). This threat came despite the fact that it was unlikely that FedEx, at the time, would be able to handle the volume of packages as convincingly as UPS. UPS and Amazon stared at each other, waiting for the opposite number to blink, but ultimately it became clear to UPS executives that Amazon was going to follow through with its threat. Thus Amazon received its preferential shipping rates.

In 2004, Amazon began selling jewellery through its website, hoping that its focus on low prices could carve a large slice out of a profitable sector. This foray was not an unambiguous success. Although it did make a profit and gave thousands of small jewellery-makers a shop window for their goods, when it came to big-ticket items with a high personalization value, such as engagement rings, it appeared that customers still valued the experience of going into a physical shop and trying on the goods, with all the glamour and reverence an online shop couldn't provide.

In the same year that Amazon launched its jewellery, however, came one of the most successful innovations in the company's history: the introduction of Amazon Prime. The idea for Prime didn't originate at senior executive level. In fact, Bezos had initiated a programme called the Idea Tool, effectively a modern version of the employee suggestion box. While Bezos is certainly an individual with strong ideas of his own, sometimes leaning head first into prevailing winds of opinion, he is also excited by the good ideas of others. One such idea came in 2004, courtesy of an engineer named Charlie Ward. In contrast to Amazon's Super Saver delivery, which gave customers the option of free delivery for orders over £25 with eligible items, Ward outlined a contrasting model, in which customers would pay a premium, as a fixed monthly fee, for permanent expedited delivery on almost everything they ordered. Bezos, ever the enthusiast for customer-oriented ideas, immediately warmed to the suggestion, which was taken to the S Team and eventually approved. Approval was not uncontested. There were many who felt that the new service would actually prove to be a cost not a profit driver. Nevertheless, Bezos was fully on board.

The new service would be known as Amazon Prime. The annual subscription price for the service was $79, the figure chosen because it was high enough to give the impression of a premium, exclusive membership, but low enough for people to give it a go without too much financial worry. Bezos later admitted that initially Prime was very expensive for the company. He likened Prime to the launch of an all-you-can-eat buffet, in which the customers who initially turn up are those who fill their plates to excess. But further behind in the queue are those with regular appetites, and once they become the majority of the customers then the buffet will start to make money. This was indeed the case with Prime. Once it had embedded itself, from around 2011, it became a roaring success. By January 2022, Amazon had more than 200 million paid Prime members globally in 24 countries. According to analysts, in the United States the service had 25 million paid members by 2013, but 99.9 million by 2017 and 142.5 million by 2020. Prime subscription fees alone were bringing in $25.21 billion in annual revenue by 2020. Furthermore, Prime has become a vehicle to build the revenues of Amazon's now mighty streaming film and TV empire, with Prime members automatically gaining access to Amazon Prime Video.

Amazon Prime was one of the more high-profile additions to the Amazon service during the mid-2000s, but there were also many other innovations around this time. For example, in 2006, Amazon introduced the Fulfilment by Amazon (FBA) programme, in which third-party suppliers could stock their goods in the Amazon FCs and have them shipped direct via Amazon's in-house fulfilment process. This gave Amazon an even broader appeal to the third-party seller market, relieving them of the onerous and costly business of having products stacked high in warehouses.

So the early years of the 2000s showed that Amazon was regaining momentum, continuing to demonstrate its boss's drive for innovation and reinvention, whatever the cost or considerations. But at the same time, there were some clouds on the horizon for both Amazon and its maverick leader. The professional turbulence that Jeff Bezos would experience and attract in the 2000s perhaps finds its metaphorical parallel in an event that occurred to Bezos on 6 March 2003. At 10 am on that date, Bezos took off in a helicopter from the base of Cathedral Mountain, West Texas, the pilot – a rough-hewn character called 'Cheater' – flying Bezos and two other passengers (Bezos' attorney Elizabeth Korrell and a cowboy guide called Ty Holland) over the Texan desert on a sightseeing trip. Cheater, a highly experienced aviator, had mounting concern during the stop-off at Cathedral Mountain, worried about the rising wind, the thin hot-and-high air and the weight of the passengers in the small helicopter, and told his passengers that they needed to take off quickly. As soon as the helicopter rose into the air, however, it was in trouble, the swirling, heated wind throwing the helicopter around as if it were a toy. It was clear that they were going down.

The helicopter smashed into the ground with force, driving one of its skids into the ground and flipping the helicopter on to its side, instantly smashing the whirling rotor blades. As it turned over, the passengers were thrown around the inside of the cabin, the helicopter eventually coming to rest partly submerged in a shallow creek called, aptly, Calamity. There were moments of crisis. Korrell was trapped underwater and under Bezos; they spotted her hand frantically signalling, Bezos moved quickly and they managed to release her from her seatbelt and get her to fresh air. She suffered broken vertebrae. The others, remarkably, escaped from the crash site with nothing more than minor cuts and some heavy bruising.

TOUGH AT THE TOP

In 1998, Stanford University students Larry Page and Sergey Brin founded Google. In the 2000s, their new approach to internet searching became the world's hottest tech story. With millions of dollars in funding and the steep revenue growth from the Google AdWords service, introduced in October 2000, the company was clearly on the up. Eric Schmidt, formerly the CEO of software company Novell and vice president at Sun Microsystems, became the new company chairman in August 2001. Gmail arrived in April 2004, the first app in what would become an increasingly powerful web-based productivity software suite, and at Google's IPO the following August, the company was valued at $23 billion.

Bezos quickly felt the rise of Google. Google now offered customers a new and powerful portal through which to search for, well, anything, including products. Furthermore, the upstart young company offered its staff a whole host of perks denied to Amazon by Bezos' more abstemious approach. Google had fun, supportive working conditions, and soon there was a worrying stream of overworked Amazon executives, some at very senior level, being tempted away to Google. This shift, and Google's rocketing presence, started to drag down Amazon's share value once again, with some analysts beginning to question both the Amazon business model and the nature of Bezos' leadership.

For Bezos, however, the rise of Google seemed only to confirm what he had always known and practised – obsessive and constant innovation are the only sure-fire ways to survive and thrive in tech-centred industries. He initiated several experiments in setting Amazon up as a rival for internet searching, but none of them gained sufficient traction to be game-changers. What Amazon needed was to find a new niche, again with huge scalable potential. Bezos, it should be noted, had never seemed driven by the desire simply to be a massive online retailer. Amazon had to be far more than that, and soon it would be.

There were some unwanted distractions, however. In 2004–5 Amazon was suddenly faced with a lawsuit from Toys "R" Us. Their claim was that Amazon was in breach of the agreement that Amazon would give Toys "R" Us exclusive rights to sell all toys on the Amazon website, even ones Toys "R" Us did not sell. In other words, Toys "R" Us maintained the agreement prohibited anyone other than themselves from selling toys in the Amazon store, even toys that Toys "R" Us didn't sell itself. The battle played itself out in a New Jersey Superior Court in September 2005, Bezos himself having to take to the witness stand for two days of very close questioning. Eventually, Amazon was compelled to settle the case for $51 million.

By many accounts, the mid years of the first decade of the 2000s were not particularly happy ones at Amazon. Set against the rise of Google, Bezos looked constantly to expand Amazon beyond its retail focus into digital services. The result was a company under ever-increasing levels of pressure, trickling down from its vigilant and impatient boss and from the people Bezos hired in to get the jobs done, some of whom were every ounce as daunting to employees as Bezos himself. The combative conditions inside the company led to more waves of discontented people leaving. They included some of Amazon's most senior and experienced figures. Two particularly significant losses were Jeff Holden, who had been the senior vice president of the company from 1997 to 2006, and Udi Manber, who joined as chief algorithms officer in

2002 and rose to senior vice president and later CEO of the A9 search subsidiary, to which we shall turn shortly. Manber's next post rubbed extra salt in the wound for Bezos – he was hired by Google in 2006 as vice president of engineering.

Amazon founded, in 2003, its own web search subsidiary, A9, which was first demonstrated on 14 April 2004 and launched the following September. It had notable features, including web and image search provided by Google, book text from Amazon. com's 'Search Inside The Book' feature, movie information from IMDb, and reference information (encyclopaedia, dictionary, etc.) through GuruNet.com. Bezos was confident in its value: 'A9.com gives people an incredible amount of power to discover information from diverse and comprehensive data sources and to manage that information effectively and easily. The search landscape is evolving at such a rapid pace that we must continue working hard to build innovative technologies that offer a great user experience.' Yet over time A9 would never be a serious challenge to Google, also a company known for rolling innovation and guided by the company mantra, 'Don't be evil'. A9 went through different types of functionality over its lifetime before the A9.com website was finally taken down in 2019.

But by then Amazon had added a quite different digital income stream, one that by 2021 was giving the company an extraordinary $62 billion of revenue and placing it at the heart of the world's internet operations. It is known as Amazon Web Services (AWS).

THE AWS REVOLUTION

AWS was born out of conflict and consultation. The conflict was the problem, felt acutely and often bitterly around 2000, of rationalizing Amazon's internal data management systems, which had become overcomplicated and internally strained due to the company's formidable growth. The streamlining of these systems focused on creating what has been called a 'shared IT platform' rather than siloed systems, so that engineers could spend more of their time working on profit-oriented, customer-focused tasks rather than infrastructure maintenance. This ultimately successful re-engineering effort coincided with a meeting in 2002 between Bezos and computer book publishing entrepreneur Tim O'Reilly. According to research by Brad Stone (based in turn on writings from O'Reilly himself), during the meeting, O'Reilly suggested to Bezos that, given Amazon's powerful market opportunities for third-party sellers and its ever-swelling databases, it should develop tools called Application Programming Interfaces (APIs) 'that allowed third parties to easily harvest data about its prices, products, and sales rankings' (Stone 2018: 241). For Bezos, this raised the possibility of third parties placing their products and services better within the Amazon digital infrastructure or even running services directly on top of the Amazon store. He took the idea back to his team to see what it could become.

APIs have been analogously likened to restaurant waiters. You, the customer (internet user), need to transfer your order from the table to the kitchen (the computer server/website that has the information you need). The waiter is essentially the API, enabling the transfer of the information to the kitchen and back to you, ensuring that you get exactly what you ordered. APIs are now sewn into our everyday web experience. They facilitate bank payments, price comparison sites, online ordering, flight booking, they connect our phones to the internet, they enable us to access maps, media and news; they mean that we can save files to directories in the cloud; they fulfil social media plugins and other dynamic content. In fact, there is little that we today do on the internet that is not facilitated by an API. Back in 2002, however, they were still in their infancy. The first web API had been introduced by Salesforce.com on 7 February 2000 and eBay launched its own API roughly nine months later. But it was still territory very much to be explored. By 2003, Amazon had built its own series of well-documented APIs.

Amazon already had some experience offering web space services to third parties through its zShops platform from the late 1990s, which enabled third-party retailers to build their own web stores upon the Amazon website. But a landmark moment came during a senior executive retreat at Bezos' house in 2003. The meeting raised the possibility of Amazon offering the scale and power of its digital infrastructure to the wider world, whose businesses could use Amazon for online storage, computing power and access to database services, rather than going to the effort and expense of installing, servicing and maintaining their own systems. Andy Jassy, a driving figure at the wheel and later head of AWS (in 2021, he would replace Bezos as the president and CEO of Amazon), later stated that, 'If you believe companies will build applications from scratch on top of the infrastructure services if the right selection [of services] existed, and we believed they would if the right selection existed, then the operating system becomes the internet, which is really different from what had been the case for the previous 30 years.'

Amazon Web Services was in fact born before the 2003 meeting. In July 2002, Amazon launched a new set of APIs that would enable developers to construct their own applications on top of Amazon, such as integrating Amazon catalogue search and payment systems within their own websites. But following the clarifying vision in 2003, AWS began its incredible climb. The detailed subsequent history of AWS is beyond this publication, but it came to embody a powerful spectrum of offerings, including Amazon S3 cloud storage launched in March 2006 (by which time more than 150,000 developers had signed up to use AWS) and Amazon Elastic Compute Cloud (EC2), launched the following August, which allowed users to rent virtual computers on which to run their own services. Other services carried names that were largely opaque to those outside the world of tech: Amazon Mechanical Turk, Amazon SimpleDB, Amazon CloudWatch, Amazon Elastic Block Store, AWS Elastic Beanstalk, Amazon Relational Database Service, Amazon DynamoDB, Amazon Simple Workflow and Amazon CloudFront. But collectively, AWS delivered results little short of awe-inspiring. By 2019, AWS constituted 12 per cent of Amazon's entire revenue and had a 39 per cent annual growth. AWS clients include the US Department of Homeland Security (DHS), the Central Intelligence Agency (CIA), the Department of Defense (DoD), the National Aeronautics and Space Administration (NASA), Netflix, numerous international governmental agencies and secret services, not to mention tens of thousands of major and minor companies and non-profits. Much of the internet as we now know it simply would not be possible were it not for AWS.

The addition of the now-mighty AWS to the already potent Amazon empire has inevitably caused controversy in places. Periodically, political questions are raised about whether tech giants such as Amazon, Apple, Alphabet (Google) and Microsoft are exercising too much influence through what some regard as de facto monopolies. Some critics have also questioned the ethical status of certain AWS clients. Amazon's relationship to the DoD Joint Enterprise Defense Infrastructure (JEDI) – a cloud computing project reputedly worth more than $10 billion over ten years – is a case in point. Many big players were initially interested in the contract, including Amazon, Google, IBM, Microsoft and Oracle. Google and IBM eventually dropped out of the race. In August 2013, Oracle filed a pre-award protest, citing three primary concerns. Two of those were related to the DoD's acquisition itself (the award structure and the procurement of future services). The third was related to alleged conflicts of interest between the DoD and AWS. (These claims were later dismissed by multiple courts and the US Government Accountability Office.) The bidding process was put on hold, a stop refreshed by President Donald Trump in August 2019, a matter of weeks before the winner was to be announced.

There was no love lost between President Trump and Jeff Bezos. Trump was a repeated critic of both Bezos and Amazon, accusing Amazon of not paying its full share of taxes and of making unfair political attacks on the Trump administration via the Bezos-owned *Washington Post*. In October 2019, the JEDI contract was awarded to Microsoft, leading to AWS filing documents with the Court of Federal Claims on 22 November 2019, challenging the decision. Unsealed court documents saw Amazon protest against 'clear deficiencies, errors, and unmistakable bias' and argue that Trump had used his political influence to swing the project away from AWS.

As a result, Microsoft's work on the JEDI project was halted when the US Court of Federal Claims concluded that Amazon was likely to succeed with its argument that the DoD improperly evaluated its proposal. On 4 September 2020, however, the DoD reaffirmed the original award to Microsoft. Notably, however, on 6 July 2021 the JEDI project was cancelled and Microsoft's contract with it. The programme, with additional requirements, evolved into the Joint Warfighter Cloud Capability (JWCC) and invitations to participate in the bid went out to four companies: Amazon, Google, Microsoft and Oracle, with the winner to be selected by the time this book goes to print in 2022.

THE PUBLISHING REVOLUTION

Bezos is a man who loves reading and books. Throughout both his academic years and his professional life, books seem to have exerted a seminal influence on his thinking, certain titles holding imaginative sway at key junctures in his life. For him, one particularly influential title was *The Innovator's Dilemma: When New Technologies Cause Great Firms to Fail* by Harvard professor and business consultant Clayton Christensen, first published in 1997. Christensen was a salutary voice in the early decades of digital tech innovation. He pondered the question of why major companies with a large market share ultimately fail. The 'dilemma' to which Christensen refers is that powerful, profitable companies sometimes have to choose between investing in a change that might ultimately destroy their existing market or sticking with the status quo of short- to medium-term secure profits, but then risk being hit by the disruptor, in the hands of a competitor, later on.

The Innovator's Dilemma became an international business bestseller; in 2011, *The Economist* even named it one of the most significant books about business ever written. Bezos read it and took its lessons to heart. Bezos' strategy for negotiating the innovator's dilemma was almost invariable – with almost iconoclastic fervour, Bezos leaned towards embracing disruption, no matter how consequential that might be for his commercial interests in the short term. In one sector in particular, books, Bezos literally remodelled an entire industry and the very way in which millions of people consume words on the page.

By 2004, when Amazon's transformation of publishing began, Bezos had already learned the hard way how a seemingly solid market could suddenly be eroded by an innovative intruder. On 9 January 2001, Apple's CEO Steve Jobs announced the arrival of iTunes, a software program that allowed users to store media, especially music, digitally. This in itself wasn't a threat to Amazon's considerable sales in music, as at this juncture in history music was largely packaged in a physical product, a CD, and Apple was not in the business of selling those. Indeed, Apple and Amazon had early discussions about the possibility of working together to optimize sales for both parties, but the negotiations did not go beyond brainstorming. Apple's market proposition, however, became more interesting in October 2001 when it launched its first-generation iPod, a portable device for storing and playing music – the days of the portable cassette tapes or CD players were truly consigned to the bin. But the real game-changer from Amazon's point of view came in April 2003, when Apple opened its iTunes Store. Now the music lover didn't even need to order a physical CD – they could just download a digital playlist from the store, save it in iTunes, and load it up on to their iPod.

Apple was not the very first to pioneer digital-only music downloads – the peer-to-peer file-sharing service Napster took that crown in the late 1990s. But whereas the copyright violations of Napster resulted in the site being shut down within a few years, Apple's iTunes Store was a phenomenal success. It had 1 million downloads in the first five days of service, and by 11 July 2004 it had sold 100 million tracks. It would go on to hit 1 billion songs sold by late February 2006.

Amazon was completely outpaced by Apple's rush into digital music, and to this day it has never entirely caught up with the music download leaders (to be fair, Apple itself would later be outpaced by nimble new arrivals, such as Spotify). But in 2004, Bezos determined that his company would take the lead in a different arena, that of electronic books (e-books).

Some had gone before him. Project Gutenberg, founded way back in 1971, had been digitizing out-of-copyright texts in increasing volumes, although the titles were only readable on a PC. Then in 1997, Martin Eberhard and Marc Tarpenning started a company called NuvoMedia, accompanied by the world's first e-reader device, known as the Rocketbook. The vision was for readers to be able to access an entire library of digitized books on a single portable device. The two young entrepreneurs needed an investor to get the product to market. They immediately thought of Amazon, and later in 1997, armed with a crude prototype of the product, they pitched it to Bezos.

The Amazon founder certainly bought into the principle and potential of the e-reader, indicated by the fact that the negotiations went on for three weeks, but he saw several major problems. He wasn't keen on the reading experience, especially the glare from the LCD screen, and he didn't like the fact that the Rocketbook needed to be connected physically to a computer to download titles;

Bezos wanted wireless downloading, a requirement that Eberhard and Tarpenning found outlandish based on the massive increase in costs of the product posed by wireless connectivity and data plans. Most crucial, however, was that Bezos wanted NuvoMedia to make an exclusive agreement with Amazon and give Amazon veto over any future investors. The thinking here was that Bezos didn't want the e-reader becoming a success and then for NuvoMedia to sell the company to Barnes & Noble further down the line. This sticking point ultimately brought all negotiations to an end, so the two young men indeed went to B&N, who bought 50 per cent of the company.

It looked like Bezos might have been outsmarted, but it was not to be. Although 20,000 Rocketbooks were sold in the first year, NuvoMedia itself struggled to acquire further funding as the dotcom bubble burst. The company was sold to TV-guide firm Gemstar, which also bought out one of the other early e-readers, Softbook. But Gemstar had problems all of its own – by 2003, Rocketbook and Softbook had gone, and B&N stopped selling the devices. Several other attempts at e-book readers, such as the EveryBook Reader and the Millennium eBook, also failed to get off the ground at this time. Maybe the world wasn't ready for e-readers.

Bezos had other ideas. Amazon already sold e-books by this time, but these products could only be viewed through Adobe or Microsoft software, plus the selection of books was limited and the prices were high. Bezos told his S Team in a meeting in 2004 that he wanted to develop a game-changing Amazon e-reader. As with many of Bezos' ideas, there was strong initial pushback, particularly from those executives who felt that for Amazon to go into manufacturing electronic products was a good way to incinerate vast amounts of R&D and manufacturing money with a high risk of failure. Undeterred, Bezos pressed on. The programme would be headed by Steve Kessel, an executive who had joined Amazon in 1999, having previously worked for Netscape. To avoid the innovator's dilemma, Bezos told Kessel that 'Your job is to kill your own business' (quoted in Stone 2018: 291), saying that Kessel should work with the urgency and focus of one actually striving to destroy the selling of printed books. Kessel, a man with almost no experience in this particular field, started recruiting and set up a secretive R&D sideline called Lab126, which was given the job of developing the Amazon-branded e-book reader. (The numbers in the title stood for letters of the alphabet, 1 = *a* and 26 = *z*, implying that the e-reader would eventually be able to access the entire A–Z library of published works.)

Lab126 had a tough brief, and one in which Bezos himself was heavily and personally interventionist. They had to incorporate wireless downloading. They had to make the device light enough for one-handed reading. The screen had to be readable in all light conditions and without inducing eye strain. The solution to this latter problem came from a system call E Ink, a type of digital paper developed by MIT undergraduates and academics in the late 1990s, which used an electrically charged field of microcapsules to generate screen images with an ocular comfort similar to that of regular printed paper. E Ink was also easy on energy consumption, giving the device the long battery life that was essential for the reader. They also had to give the device a code name, and they opted for 'Fiona', a character in Neal Stephenson's *The Diamond Age*, a novel with a plot line revolving around an interactive textbook.

But later, graphic designer and marketing consultant Michael Cronan was brought into the branding process. He gave the device the name that stuck and that became virtually synonymous with e-books – Kindle.

To give the product a physically attractive and marketable form, Lab126 hired the services of international design company Pentagram, specifically their San Francisco office. They also had to wrestle with Bezos' interventions. One of the biggest battles was fought over the inclusion of a physical keyboard built into the device, something that Pentagram resisted, seeing the keyboard as spoiling the clean lines of the device. Bezos overruled them forcibly in several tense meetings (Stone 2018: 296). Eventually, the design of the product passed back to Lab126 and the finalized product design and specifications were agreed. Then came the matter of manufacturing, which in itself threw up a veritable hurdle course of obstacles that stretched out the product launch further and further.

But there was another issue that needed addressing, and it was a big one. Bezos announced to his team that his goal for the Kindle upon launch was for readers to be able to access and download a library of no fewer than 100,000 titles, including 90 per cent of all the *New York Times'* bestsellers. The trouble was, the world's publishers had only digitized about 20,000. It was time for Amazon to use all its considerable muscle to lean on the publishers to digitize their stock. But why would they want to do this? For most, indeed all, publishers at this time, e-books were a tiny niche product line – their profits came from printed and bound volumes, offering an experience of reading that would be recognizable if a modern book were transported back to ancient times. Furthermore, why would they want to generate digital versions of their books if these products would, by being sold cheaper than the physical product, undercut their main line of business?

Thus began one of the most controversial developmental episodes in Amazon's history, a time in which once again Bezos unswervingly remained locked on to the customer offer – all other considerations were secondary. Bezos hired a tough negotiator, Lyn Blake – someone who had worked in the commercial book sector – to squeeze the publishers to reduce the wholesale price of books to Amazon. This began from around 2004, and all publishers, large and small, came into the crosshairs. Resist, and the publisher risked its works being cut from Amazon's recommendation algorithms, which considering that the bulk of the world's books was now being sold through Amazon could have a serious impact on sales, possibly resulting in the collapse of the company. Meet the demands for discounts, and the publisher's profits, and by implication those of the authors, could be painfully squeezed. It was not a good time for publisher–Amazon relations. Brad Stone revealed that the scheme was termed the Gazelle Program, based on the fact that Bezos had explained the project to Blake in terms of Amazon being a cheetah and each publisher looking like a lone and vulnerable gazelle. (Blake left Amazon in 2005.)

Then there was the matter of e-books. Digitizing existing titles was a practical and legal headache for publishers, and without a clear sense of a strong emerging market they had little incentive to do so. In 2006, Amazon started revealing the tool that would create that market, when it started to show publishers the Fiona/Kindle prototype, something that Amazon had diligently kept secret up to this point. At first, many publishers were distinctly underwhelmed by what was then still a rather clunky device. But with the possibility of wireless connectivity, the Kindle started to receive more buy-in from the publishers, and the volumes of digitized books steadily rose, incentivized by some pressure from Amazon about the consequences if they didn't produce e-books fast enough.

Jeff Bezos launched the Kindle on 19 November 2007 at the W Hotel in Lower Manhattan, to an audience of journalists and publishing executives. By this time, Amazon had built a library of their intended 100,000 e-books, and 25,000 boxed Kindles were sitting in the Amazon FCs, ready for shipment. All the customer had to do to get hold of an e-book was to order one through their regular Amazon account and the product would be delivered

Jeff Bezos holds aloft the new Amazon tablet called the Kindle Fire on 28 September 2011 in New York City. During the following December, Amazon sold more than one million Kindle devices every week.

wirelessly, and instantly, to their device. It sold for $399 and each device could hold literally hundreds of publications. It was a true revolution in publishing.

The launch event brought an unpleasant surprise to already jittery and bruised publishing executives, when Bezos announced a flat rate price of $9.99 for all *New York Times* bestsellers and new releases. This sent a ripple throughout the room, it being the first time the publishers had heard of the pricing model. Given that a new hardback might be priced at $25 or more, the $9.99 e-book offer massively undercut the printed titles.

It was the beginning of a long, bitter battle between Bezos, Amazon and publishers over pricing. It would lead, in time, to several major court battles. The first came in 2011, when Amazon sued Apple and the world's 'Big Five' publishers – Hachette, HarperCollins, Simon & Schuster, Penguin (later Penguin-Random House) and Macmillan – for conspiring to fix e-book charges. Amazon won its case, with the publishers ultimately paying out $166 million in damages while Apple received a bill to consumers for $400 million. But in a strange reversal, in 2021, the law firm Hagens Berman – in a supreme irony the same law firm that represented Amazon over the 2011 case – filed a class-action lawsuit against Amazon and the Big Five for colluding to inflate e-book pricing on platforms other than Amazon's own. At the time of writing, this case has yet to go through the courts.

But winding back in time, and for now sidelining the controversies, the Kindle added yet another powerful profit engine to Amazon. It had an early hiccup: the entire stock of Kindles sold out in just five-and-a-half hours and it wasn't back in stock again until April 2008. But after that, sales of Kindles, thereafter released in improved models, and e-books took off and soared. By the end of 2009, about 1.5 million Kindles had been sold. Other major players, including B&N, attempted to catch up, but by 2010 Amazon had 48 per cent of the market. The sales of the Kindle delivered huge revenues – an estimated $3.57 billion in 2012 and $5 billion in 2014, to select just two years.

Bezos was ebullient about the Kindle in his 2007 letter to shareholders. After explaining the consumer rush to buy the Kindle, and the features of the new device, Bezos gave something of a potted history of the evolution of reading, from the invention of Gutenberg's printing press in 1440 to the launch of the Kindle. Within this discourse, he reveals some important details about how he views the absorption of information in the present age. Despite being a tech believer, Bezos negatively reflects on the way that modern digital devices have increasingly pushed us towards what he calls 'information snacking', grazing constantly on snippets of facts and data, the process of which drives us towards shorter attention spans. As we shall explore in our final chapter, Bezos does not appreciate lax or superficial thinking – an executive who based his corporate ideas on 'information snacking' would likely have a rough and intimidating ride in a Bezos meeting. Interestingly, Bezos sees the Kindle as a corrective to shallow thought, a device that encourages 'long-form reading' and acts as a cognitive corrective: 'We hope Kindle and its successors may gradually and incrementally move us over the years into a world with longer spans of attention, providing a counterbalance to the recent proliferation of info-snacking tools. I realize my tone here tends toward the missionary, and I can assure you it's heartfelt.'

But the advent of Kindle and its fast delivery of e-books was not the only transformation that Bezos and Amazon wrought in the world of book publishing. Concurrent with the launch of the Kindle, Amazon announced the launch of a new self-publishing service for authors, called Digital Text Platform in 2007 but eventually retitled Kindle Direct Publishing (KDP). KDP broke wide open the traditional model between author and publishing (or between author, agent and publisher). Through KDP, anyone could write a book and publish it as an e-book or (through an additional Amazon service called CreateSpace, a company acquired by Amazon in 2005) a print-on-demand paperback, and then sell it through the Amazon store. Unlike publisher royalty rates, which typically gravitated around 5–15 per cent of net sales, the author of a KDP publication could be netting 35 per cent or 70 per cent of the cover price, depending on the options for sale selected. Amazon had now made it even more viable for aspiring and even established authors to publish their own works directly, cutting out the publisher in the process.

This was a revolutionary model for publishing. Of course, it wasn't as simple as it sounded. As with all self-published works, the quality was extremely variable and as in regular publishing, only a rare few managed to earn something approaching a living out of it. But it was still another cause for concern for the publishing industry. E-book self-publishing became, within the space of a decade, a $1 billion industry, and much of this growth was laid at the door of Amazon; in 2016, some 40 per cent of the 4 million e-books released by Amazon were self-published, and royalties to KDP authors had climbed to $900 million by 2019. In his 2011 letter to shareholders, Bezos gave space to self-published KDP authors to recount how the service had changed their lives, providing them with intellectual freedom, removing barriers to market and transforming their earnings from their writings. Bezos used such accounts as a springboard to explain how 'invention has become second nature' at Amazon.

CHAPTER 5
AMAZON EVERYWHERE

In the decade beginning 2010, the world's perception of both Bezos and Amazon changed irrevocably. Amazon entered the new decade undoubtedly a leading figure in the world of e-commerce, but there were still question marks over long-term profitability. On a talk show in 2014, Steve Ballmer, the CEO of Microsoft, referred to Amazon as a 'Nice company' but one that wasn't really making money. Six years later, such viewpoints would appear almost comically outdated. Amazon's revenue figures, graphed over the decade, showed an extraordinary growth pattern, the bar chart looking like the flat run then the precipitous climb (from 2015) at the beginning of a roller-coaster ride. At the end of 2010, Amazon recorded annual net sales of $33.4 billion, with a net income of $1.15 billion. In 2021, by stratospheric contrast, the annual revenue was nearly $470 billion, with a net income of $33.4 billion. And remember, the 2021 figures were recorded after the world had endured two years of one of the worst global crises since the Second World War, the Covid-19 pandemic. Without downplaying the human cost of the pandemic, this international calamity actually worked to Amazon's commercial advantage, as its retail arm became a lifeline to millions of home-bound people across the world, while the switch to online working and selling fed AWS with even more commercial calories. Incredibly, Amazon's annual revenue rose 37.62 per cent in 2020 and another 21.7 per cent in 2021.

As Amazon swelled, so did Bezos' personal financial profile, a fact that gripped the attention of the media. His net worth topped $150 billion in 2018 and went above $200 billion just two years later. But whereas many initially innovative companies suddenly ran out of steam and fell behind energetic newcomers during the 2000s, Amazon simply kept straining into the wind, led by a boss who was never satisfied with anything approaching the status quo. Thus the inventions kept on coming, some of them self-destructing well before they reached commercial orbit, others ultimately taking great slabs of market share in territory in which few had ever even contemplated the intrusion of the e-commerce empire.

FIRE AND ECHOES

It is clear from our journey with Bezos so far that his mercurial ideas did not all hit home runs. Many, in fact, quickly ran through

Jeff Bezos speaks to new Amazonians at a New Hire Orientation Day in September 2019. Today, Amazon supports more than 4 million workers around the world.

their three strikes and were consigned to the bin. One that deserves a special mention is the Amazon Fire smartphone, not least because almost no one owns one any more, unless as a forgotten relic in a dusty drawer.

By 2010, Bezos felt tense as he viewed the rise of the smartphone, as the likes of Google, Apple and Samsung carved up the new and exponentially accelerating market between them. Fearing the possibility of being sidelined by others' innovation, Bezos commissioned 'Project B', which would then come under the code name 'Tyto' (named after a genus of owl) and ultimately the product name it launched under, Fire Phone.

There was a complementary logic to developing a smartphone. In November 2011, Amazon launched the Kindle Fire tablet, a modestly priced competitor to the high-end Apple iPad. Although the Fire tablet would not knock the iPad from its pole position, it did become a strong competitor in the tablet market and remains a popular tablet option to this day. But back in the early 2010s, it likely seemed to Bezos that without a smartphone, Amazon was ceding ground, and that was plainly unacceptable.

The development programme for the Fire Phone was protracted and tortuous. From the outset, Bezos had a vision for the device as a square-on competitor to the iPhone, with ultra-sophisticated features such as a 3D display and motion control by gestures rather than purely on-screen taps. The engineer teams struggled to fulfil such a demanding brief, particularly the 3D display, which quickly sucked the life out of contemporary battery technologies. Brad Stone also recounts an occasion when Bezos apparently expressed incredulity that anyone used a calendar feature on their phones, with several Amazon employees having to convince him that they did (Stone 2021: 39). The project became increasingly complex and branched into two strands: one the high-end device that would become the Fire Phone, and another low-cost version labelled 'Otus', which was eventually dropped, even though some in Amazon believed that Otus represented a better opportunity to gain smartphone market share.

Finally, after endless successive delays, the Fire Phone had its launch on 18 June 2014, Bezos revealing the new device to the world's media at a presentation in the Fremont Theater in Seattle. Critical responses to the phone were decidedly mixed, tending towards the lukewarm or outright disappointed. Some tech analysts appreciated the innovation or quality of specific features but regarded the total package and pricing as not attractive enough to draw users away from Android and Mac OS phones. They were right. Amazon enjoyed a burst of Fire Phone sales for about two weeks before they entered a death spiral, one that couldn't be arrested by price reductions or further service sweeteners. Within a year, the Fire Phone had been discontinued, Amazon having taken a $170 million hit in its development.

The salutary failure of the Fire Phone has to be laid, in largest measure, at the feet of Jeff Bezos himself. His involvement in the minutiae of the development phase was, according to some, obsessive and unhelpful. Yet Bezos has always accepted the risks of innovation as well as the rewards, and he has never been mute about acknowledging the Fire Phone's failure. But as if demonstrating the wisdom of Canadian-American scientist Oswald Avery's motto, 'Whenever you fall, pick something up', Bezos did not leave the Fire Phone without a gain, as he explained in his 2018 letter to shareholders: 'Development of the Fire phone and Echo was started around the same time. While the Fire phone was a failure, we were able to take our learnings (as well as the developers) and accelerate our efforts building Echo and Alexa.'

The story of Echo and Alexa – respectively the Amazon interactive speaker and its soft-voiced virtual assistant – connects Amazon with the snowballing interest in the world of Artificial Intelligence (AI), systems in which computers 'think' in more flexible and human-like ways, the thinking ever refined by the continual input of data from the users. The vision for Echo began around the same time as that for the Fire Phone, 2010, when Bezos started looking into the possibilities of voice-activated devices, allied with AI. (Actually, we could say that his interest really goes back to his childhood fondness for the interactive speaking computer aboard the USS *Enterprise* in *Star Trek*.) By 2010, such systems were already in commercial operation, particularly in some brands of smartphone and in voice-controlled computer and dictation software. Bezos roughly mapped a vision for the device, which would sit in a home or office running through the wireless network, picking up voice commands via an inbuilt microphone. In return, the users would get whatever they requested within the parameters of the device – travel information, weather reports, music, etc. The job of developing what could be, on first impressions, another of Bezos' 'fever dreams' was given to Lab126, more specifically a team headed by Greg Hart, an executive who had been with Amazon since 2009.

The development of the future Echo and Alexa would be one of the more challenging technical feats in Amazon's history, an effort that rode on the cutting edge of human/computer interaction. Amazon was compelled to acquire several leading tech start-ups, including the Polish company Ivona, founded in 2001 and specializing in human-sounding computer-generated speech. Given the diversity of queries Alexa might have to field, it could not be based around pre-set recordings; Ivona had developed a system whereby the computer could form new words by digitally combining sound fragments from an actual human voice.

By 2013, the work, running under the code name 'Doppler', had yielded the first iteration of the Echo device, in its characteristic upright 'Pringles can' format, featuring integrated microphone and speakers. To awaken the device, the users simply had to say the word 'Alexa' and make their request. But getting the speaker to recognize all the nuances and idiosyncrasies of human speech proved to be a mighty hill to climb, especially in collecting the volume of speech data required. At first, the devices were tested in the homes of obliging Amazon employees, but this wasn't enough to build the data set. The problem was cracked, however, by an ingenious sub-project called AMPED, run by an Australian data collection company, in which Alexa devices were planted in numerous rented homes and apartments, properties that had a high turnover of workers and occupants plus thousands of paid volunteers, all bringing their distinctive speech patterns. With the devices running around the clock, the massive data set resulting from AMPED (all collected consensually, it should be added) gave Amazon a strident boost in the field of voice recognition software.

As with other important projects, Bezos was personally involved from the outset, commenting on elements such as the brightness of the device's glowing recognition light and calling for complex interactions between Alexa and the Fire Tablet. Not all the calls he made, in retrospect, proved right for the product, but his guiding energy still ensured that the product went through to launch, on 6 November 2016.

Unlike the Fire Phone, Alexa and Echo genuinely was the beginning of a new movement in home technology. Alexa somehow managed to merge sci-fi futurity with comforting familiarity, and properly used could be genuinely and instinctively useful. Critical feedback from the press was good and the customer waiting list was long – more than 300,000 devices were on immediate order. The flywheel began to spin once again, and good sales became phenomenal sales – by 2019, more than 100 million Echo devices had been sold worldwide. In his 2018 statement to shareholders, Bezos explained an important ingredient to innovation, namely that existing customer needs are not always a good guide:

> No customer was asking for Echo. This was definitely us wandering. Market research doesn't help. If you had gone to a customer in 2013 and said 'Would you like a black, always-on cylinder in your kitchen about the size of a Pringles can that you can talk to and ask questions, that also turns on your lights and plays music?' I guarantee you they'd have looked at you strangely and said, 'No, thank you.'

Another key driver behind the popularity of Amazon Echo has been Amazon's increasing power in the arena of digital music. Amazon launched its MP3 online music store in September 2007 as a public beta in the United States. A crucial USP in the service was that the music was offered without digital rights management (DRM), which meant that users could freely copy the tracks, including those from major labels such as EMI, Universal, Warner and Sony BMG. Apple also subsequently secured these rights and Brad Stone noted that thereafter 'Amazon remained a perennial straggler in music' (Stone 2018: 286). Amazon then launched its music streaming service, Amazon Music, in 2014.

Yet the situation is changing. While Amazon Music still trails the likes of Apple Music and Spotify, its growth has outpaced them. In early 2020 the company announced more than 55 million subscribers and an annual growth rate of more than 30 per cent. It has some distance to go to catch the likes of Spotify (*c*. 180 million paid subscribers), but it remains a major contender in the digital music market.

AMAZON ON SCREEN

Looking across the Amazon portfolio, one of the more surprising diversions that Bezos followed was taking the company into TV and film production. Making TV series and full-length movies is a world apart from e-commerce, more the province of the big Hollywood studios or the primetime TV production companies, which stacked up decades of experience and market understanding. Yet undaunted, Bezos launched Amazon into this new arena, and thrived there. Amazon's creative output has today made it a regular winner or nominee at the Oscars, Academy Awards and major film festivals, in multiple language categories. Films such as *Manchester by the Sea* (2016), *The Salesman* (2017), *You Were Never Really Here* (2017), *Cold War* (2018), *Honey Boy* (2019) and *Being the Ricardos* (2021), and TV series such as *Sneaky Pete* (premiered 2015), *The Man in the High Castle* (2015) and *The Romanoffs* (2018) have attracted both critical acclaim and big-name stars. The output from Amazon Studios and Amazon Prime

Video is seriously respected and, with classic disruptive effect, a source of concern for many traditional studios.

The spur for Bezos to go into TV and film was, in one word, Netflix. Founded in 1997 by Reed Hastings and Marc Randolph in Scotts Valley, California, Netflix began live selling and renting DVDs via mail, but in 2007, fuelled by the expanding access to high-speed broadband internet, it moved into streaming video on demand (SVOD). Such was its success in this field that it had the money and the will to go into content production in 2013, launching this effort with the widely celebrated series *House of Cards*. Today, it is one of the largest media production companies in the world, with more than 220 million subscribers and a simple model – for a monthly subscription, you get full access to everything in the Netflix library.

Back in 2010, Bezos witnessed the rise of Netflix and knew it was time for Amazon to take a slice of the SVOD market. His concept was called Prime Video. The idea was that Amazon Prime customers could get access to SVOD content through their existing account; in a sense, Prime Video would be a free addition to an existing service. Bezos allocated $30 million to develop the idea, which would be practically handled by Bill Carr, the executive in charge of Amazon's digital music and video.

The new service opened for business on 7 September 2006, initially known as Amazon Unbox in the United States, later Amazon Video on Demand and Amazon Prime Video. The driving force behind the creative content of Prime Video was the aggressive pursuit of licensing deals with media companies, production studios and TV networks to broadcast their most popular shows. Deals were signed with Viacom, Cinemax, Discovery Channel,

Showtime, Sony Pictures, PBS, Boomerang and more. Output grew impressively – by 2014, Amazon were offering 40,000 video titles.

Yet parallel to Prime Video building its catalogue of externally produced content, there was also a cautiously excited investigation of the possibility of Amazon making its own films and shows. The seed of the idea had been planted by Amazon executive Roy Price, who joined the company in 2004 to develop a digital video strategy. As Price and Carr worked together to build a vision of possibilities, Bezos gave his unique take on the way forward, again looking to place innovative distance between Amazon and traditional ways of bringing entertainment to the masses. His vision was for 'the scientific studio', a process in which anyone could send in a script idea, not just agent-represented and studio-approved scriptwriters. The ideas would be assessed by customers, Amazon staff and independent judges with the promise of feedback to the writer within 90 days. This way, the commissioning process would be informed by data and a customer's preferences, rather than the often misguided personal judgement of a media producer. The scientific studio was tested out from 2010, but Bezos' hopes of democratizing the commissioning process ran up against a deluge of poor-quality scripts, and thus the focus turned back to direct work with professional scriptwriters, scrutinized or commissioned by Amazon executives. The vehicle for producing the shows that made it through the vetting process was Amazon Studios, founded on 16 November 2010.

In April 2013, Amazon made available pilot screenings of 14 different shows produced by Amazon Studios, with the comedies *Betas*, *Alpha House* and *Annedroids* surviving the pilot and premiering later in the year. Feedback on the shows was generally positive, but unexceptional, however, and Bezos and Price looked for routes to greater public traction. Led by Price, the decision was taken to focus on developing distinctly high-quality programming inspired by indie films, giving Amazon customers cosmopolitan and polished content that separated Amazon from the run of predictable box-ticking shows filling the majority of schedules. It was an inspired vision, one that would give Prime Video a coherent and appealing brand. Well-received shows such as *Transparent* (2014), *Mozart in the Jungle* (2014) and *Bosch* (2015) showcased the new approach (*Transparent* was the first SVOD production to win Golden Globe awards), and thereafter the trajectory was up, even in a market with increased competition for SVOD viewers. In 2020, for example, Amazon spent $11 billion on movies, TV and music, an investment growth of 41 per cent compared to the previous year. The ease of accessing the content was driven harder by the introduction, in 2014, of the Amazon Fire Stick, a memory-stick-sized network device that, once plugged into the side of a TV set, allows users to stream content effortlessly from router to TV.

And people were not only watching and reading Amazon content. Amazon Audible, an online audio book and podcast service, had also grown impressively since its launch way back in 1997, and had become the world's largest seller and producer of audiobooks. In his 2013 letter to shareholders, Bezos was rapturous over the Audible service:

> Audible customers downloaded close to six hundred million listening hours in 2013. Thanks to Audible Studios, people drive to work listening to Kate Winslet, Colin Firth, Anne Hathaway, and many other stars. One big hit in 2013 was Jake Gyllenhaal's

performance of *The Great Gatsby*, which has already sold one hundred thousand copies. Whispersync for Voice allows customers to switch seamlessly back and forth between reading a book on their Kindle and listening to the corresponding Audible book on their smart phone.

Alongside Echo and Alexa, alongside the packages arriving on doorsteps, alongside the AWS infrastructure running in the background of much digital life, Amazon was now even more present in the daily digital lives of citizens around the world. But Bezos also began moves to make Amazon not just a digital presence, but a force built in bricks and mortar.

AMAZON STORES

Bezos formed Amazon to transform the possibilities of retail. Amazon was the alternative to the physical store, a vast, borderless shopping experience that brought the goods to the customer rather than the customer to the goods. Amazon's disruptive effect on the retail landscape was as much to do with defying traditional models as it was to do with defining the contours of the new world of e-commerce. It is therefore curious that in 2012 Bezos began discussions with his senior team regarding the prospect of Amazon opening physical stores. But what at first glance might seem to be an ill-advised move to compete on the high street, was actually another attempt to rewrite the rules.

Driving Bezos' thinking was the convergence of three principal technical threads. First, the processing power available for computing had increased stratospherically since 1994, raising new vistas of automation and data processing. Second, real-time pattern-recognition video cameras had become a reality. Third, AI and deep learning were by now really showing their muscle and potential, in fields ranging from playing chess to industrial robotics. Bezos took these factors and suggested that his executives investigate ways in which high-end technology could change the very nature of a physical store. A team was appointed, led by Steve Kessel (the man who had taken the Kindle to market), and they began the journey under the frequent scrutiny of their energetic and fascinated boss, but also under conditions of high secrecy.

What emerged was encapsulated in a single catchphrase: 'Just Walk Out' (JWO) technology. It was an extraordinary idea. The principle was that customers would enter the store and identify themselves on entry. (Access identification has been achieved using an in-store code on the Amazon shopping app or, at select Amazon Go store locations, by using Amazon One – a contactless identification system using the customer's palm – or credit card.) Once inside, the customers would do their shopping, then walk straight out without going through a physical checkout, payment being automatically deducted. The store technology – hundreds of cameras and weight sensors, linked to banks of supercomputers – would track each customer's every move, every product selection (including items put back or changed), and accurately tally up the whole basket on exit, billing the customer's Amazon account. There would be nothing else like it. It would be called Amazon Go.

Amazon Go was a scintillating idea, and one that Bezos quickly embraced and funded. It was decided to focus the project on selling groceries in a mid-sized convenience store format (at first the proposition included fresh produce, but that was later dropped). But technologically there were mountains to climb, and vast amounts of money to spend on R&D. From initial discussions in 2012, it took five years to bring the project to a launch to the public. The conceptual and practical challenges seemed endless as it was quickly realized how problematic it was for computers and cameras to model and track the variables of human actions and environmental changes. The developers had to account for lighting conditions, clothing, hesitancy, objects that looked like products, breakages, variable sizes of products, and a multitude of other factors. The erratic and irrational behaviour of small children accompanying the shoppers, for example, required vast digital effort to distinguish from the meaningful action of shoppers. A test store was constructed in a warehouse in Seattle, which Bezos eagerly tried out in front of a nervous development team, his principal feedback being that the customer experience needed to be slicker.

Amazon Go did not have the easiest of births. The first store opened in December 2016, but only to Amazon employees so the system could be tested and proven before the launch to the public a few weeks later. Such was the magnitude of the issues, however, that the first public store would not open until January 2018. When it did, however, the press was stunned by the implications of the concept. The reactions at that time ranged from celebrations at a new form of liberated shopping to dismay at future visions of the technology resulting in cashiers being made redundant. Amazon countered the latter concern by stating that store employees are still an important part of the store experience. With the use of Just Walk Out technology, they shifted how store employees spent their time in order to focus on activities that improve the customer experience such as stocking inventory or greeting customers at the door.

According to a Bloomberg article in 2018, Amazon was aiming to open several thousand Amazon Go stores over the next three years (Spencer Soper, 'Amazon Will Consider Opening Up to 3,000 Cashierless Stores by 2021'; 19 September 2018), although this assertion can't be confirmed as being by Bezos himself. By March 2021 more than 20 had been opened. Given the investment of time and money that had been sunk into project R&D, it might be classed as one of Bezos' major failures. But if we have learned anything from Amazon and Bezos, the passage of time and the later maturation of a market or technology can change the picture significantly, so we wait and see. Nor is Amazon Go the company's only chain of stores. In November 2015, for example, Amazon opened the first of its Amazon Books stores (again in Seattle), selling popular Amazon titles plus a selection of Amazon electronic devices. (In March 2022, however, Amazon announced it was closing all these stores.) It opened Amazon Fresh, a grocery delivery service, in the United States in 2007, and has since launched physical stores under the name in the United States and United Kingdom, some of them utilizing the JWO technology. (As a clarification, some Amazon Fresh US stores use JWO technology, but all stores internationally use JWO.) A true eyebrow-raiser came in 2017, when Amazon purchased the Whole Foods Market supermarket chain for more than $13 billion, a move that sent tremors through the grocery industry. In his shareholder letter, Bezos explained some of the innovations Amazon brought to the 40-year-old Whole Foods: lower prices on popular lines and staples; exclusive promotions for Prime members, including two-hour delivery on orders in select cities, and 5 per cent back for those shopping at Whole Foods Market with a Prime Rewards VISA credit card; free grocery pickup for orders over $35 from Whole Foods Market stores; exclusive deals and an additional 10 per cent off all sale items (excluding alcohol) at Whole Foods Market. Looking to the future, Amazon also offers retailers the ability to use its JWO technology, showing yet again how Amazon continues to be a platform for third-party retailers. Industry analysts with a critical eye spoke warily of how, in the future, Amazon might wield all the customer and product data it was collecting via Whole Foods.

By the beginning of the 2020s, the Amazon empire had once again bulked out that bit more, growing as if through a process of endless cellular division. But as Amazon pressed on into the decade, it would not be Bezos himself at the wheel.

MOVING ON

In February 2021, Jeff Bezos announced that he was stepping down as Amazon's CEO, passing the role into the safe hands of long-term Amazon executive Andy Jassy the following July. The press coverage of this landmark event inevitably focused on the fact that Bezos had, from scratch, built a company that had transformed his personal fortunes from being a wide-eyed young entrepreneur predicting a 70 per cent chance of failure for his ventures, to being officially crowned as the world's richest man, with a total net worth of $203 billion at the time of his leaving.

Bezos wasn't quitting Amazon entirely, in fact, far from it. Holding just over 10 per cent of Amazon shares, he was the largest shareholder in the company, plus he was moving into the position of Amazon's executive chair. So, combined with his cultural influence on the company, he still had a powerful say over Amazon's future direction. This being said, Bezos had also developed absorbing new interests outside Amazon by 2021, especially his Blue Origin spaceflight programme (see Chapter 6) and the various intellectual, research and philanthropic activities that he pursued through Bezos Expeditions (see Chapter 7), such as the acquisition of the *Washington Post*. His email to employees explained his reasons thus:

> Being the CEO of Amazon is a deep responsibility, and it's consuming. When you have a responsibility like that, it's hard to put attention on anything else. As Exec Chair, I will stay engaged in important Amazon initiatives but also have the time and energy I need to focus on the Day 1 Fund, the Bezos Earth Fund, Blue Origin, the *Washington Post*, and my other passions. I've never had more energy, and this isn't about retiring.

We should remember that Bezos had by now turned 58 years old and was still handling a portfolio of demanding interests that would have burned out most 23-year-olds. Whatever his move away from Amazon was, it was certainly nothing approaching a retirement.

Much had changed for Bezos personally as well as professionally by the time of his leaving Amazon. Many people noted how physically fit he had become – lean, toned and healthy – the product of a disciplined regime of healthy eating and working out. An article on *Men's Health* website in July 2017 bore the title 'Amazon CEO Jeff Bezos Is Now Buff; Internet Freaks Out', posting 'before and after' style photos to highlight the transformation from willowy tech geek to a man in 'crazy good shape'. Bezos was also seen socializing a lot more than during his early days of success, often seen on red carpets or rubbing shoulders with celebrities, politicians, fellow billionaires and other high-flyers.

One of the biggest changes in Bezos' personal life, though, came in January 2019, when Bezos announced that he and his wife of 25 years, MacKenzie, were filing for divorce. The following day, the *National Enquirer* ran a lengthy story regarding an affair between Bezos and Lauren Sánchez, a beautiful and high-profile entertainment reporter, news anchor and businesswoman. Bezos had been seeing Sánchez, who was also married (to Patrick Whitesell, a talent agency executive), since 2018, the same year in which the *National Enquirer* began investigating the story. The full story of this intensely personal drama, which become increasingly public the following year, is told in most detail by Brad Stone in his follow-up work to *The Everything Store*, titled *Amazon Unbound*, but the legal and political drama that subsequently unfolded is worth outlining, if only for how Bezos' personal life could capture the attention of the world. Chapter 7 looks at this story in more detail, but we should here say that MacKenzie went on to continued success in her own right, and according to the press also became the world's third-richest woman from the divorce settlement (she would go on to divest much of her wealth through philanthropy).

CHAPTER 6
BEZOS BEYOND – BLUE ORIGIN

On 20 July 2021, Blue Origin – the space company founded by Jeff Bezos 21 years previously – issued a rather dry press release about what was, in reality, a momentous event both in the history of spaceflight and in the personal life of Bezos himself:

> Blue Origin successfully completed *New Shepard's* first human flight today with four private citizens onboard. The crew included Jeff Bezos, Mark Bezos, Wally Funk and Oliver Daemen, who all officially became astronauts when they passed the Kármán Line, the internationally recognized boundary of space. Upon landing, the astronauts were greeted by their families and Blue Origin's ground operations team for a celebration in the West Texas desert.

It was a day of firsts aboard *New Shepard*. Mary Wallace 'Wally' Funk, a veteran American aviator, was at the age of 82 the oldest person ever to venture into space. Eighteen-year-old Dutch citizen Oliver Daemen was, by contrast, the youngest person to go into space, and also the first customer to fly on *New Shepard* – he bought a ticket to fly on a private space vehicle, launched from a private space facility. Jeff and Mark Bezos, meanwhile, were space exploration's first siblings to make a joint spaceflight together. Most

Blue Origin's first human flight crew celebrate at the landing pad alongside the New Shepard *booster on 20 July 2021. Left to right: Oliver Daemen, Jeff Bezos, Wally Funk, Mark Bezos.*

crucially, however, Jeff Bezos, the man who as a child had dreamt of being an astronaut, had punched beyond Earth's atmosphere and gone into the black heavens beyond. Incredibly, he did so in a spacecraft built by his own space company, funded out of his own purse and developed according to his own vision of beyond-Earth futures. In the post-flight press conference, Bezos, wearing a now-signature cowboy hat, reflected on what the mission meant but also on the message that this was not a one-off vanity launch, but the beginning of a great journey into the future:

What practice does is lets you get better ... Right now we have a mission life, we think, somewhere between 25 and 100 flights for one of these vehicles. We'd like to make that closer to 100 than to 25. Then once it's close to 100, we will push it past 100. That's how you get operational usability. You have to remember, big things start small. I told this crew when we got in today and we were sitting there on the pad waiting to lift off. We had time to ourselves and I just said, 'Guys, if you're willing, if you let me invite you, when we get up there, there's going to be all kinds of adrenaline, all kinds of excitement and novelty, but take a minute, take a few seconds to look out and calmly think about what we're doing is not only adventure. It is adventure and it is fun, but it's also important because what we're doing is the first step of something big.'

The *New Shepard* launch was indeed 'the first step of something big', the beginning of a new age in space exploration. For decades in the United States, space flight had been almost exclusively the purview of NASA, a vast government entity. Now Bezos – a private individual, albeit one of the richest men on the planet – was taking a slice of space real estate on his own coin and with his own facilities, staff and innovations. For Bezos, it evidently seemed that despite all that he had achieved in his earthbound career, Earth was no longer enough.

THE LAUNCH PAD

Bezos founded Blue Origin in 2000. It says much for Bezos' optimistic psychology and intellectual capacity that he did this at a time when his plate was surely very full dealing with the financial challenges of a staggering dotcom sector. The company established its HQ in Seattle, and one of its first employees – indeed the person who actually encouraged Bezos to found the organization – was Neal Town Stephenson. Stephenson was a successful novelist, working in science fiction, historical fiction, cyberpunk and other genres, but was also an expert in science and technology. Others were steadily brought in, individuals with cutting-edge expertise in all matters relating to spaceflight, and who could help Bezos break through traditional models of how travelling beyond Earth was conducted. One of the newcomers was aerospace engineer Rob Meyerson, a specialist in space launch systems – he was hired as a member of the engineering staff and was named president in 2003.

In a vibrant think tank atmosphere, Bezos and the group let free thinking reign as they attempted to envisage a new era in space exploration. A core focus for Bezos was that crewed space flight had to achieve entirely new frameworks of efficiency if it was to become more than highly intermittent launches from government-owned facilities, each launch being accompanied by vast costs, slow turnarounds and often the loss of one-time space components (such as engines and boosters). Bezos was fixated on the possibilities for truly reusable spacecraft that would, one day, be able to fly to and from space in a manner similar to that of a commercial jet. All ideas were on the table.

Blue Origin was founded without fanfare, and for many years the project was well hidden from public view. But as well as the intellectual investigations of space exploration, Bezos began making the practical steps required to realize the project. In 2003–4, he began buying up land in West Texas, quietly acquiring ranches and other plots of desert land until he had some 290,000 open, arid acres. The land was purchased through lawyers under code names, in the attempt to shield his new investments from public eyes. It would eventually become Launch Site One – the launch site for Blue Origin spacecraft, located about 40 km (25 miles) from the town of Van Horn. The story began to leak out, however, not least through the work of investigative journalist Brad Stone (the later author of two of the most comprehensive studies of Bezos and Amazon). In 2003, following some alleged discoveries made in the waste bin outside Blue Origin's registered office, Stone published an article in *Newsweek* entitled 'Bezos in Space'. It revealed core elements of the Blue Origin vision – the desire to create durable colonies in space; the building of a reusable spacecraft called *New Shepard*, with vertical take-off and landing operation; new designs for space launch technologies; giving tourists access to spaceflight. The choice of name for the new spacecraft was resonant. It was named after Alan Bartlett Shepard Jr., the first American to travel into space as part of NASA's Mercury programme; he was also involved in the Apollo programme, walking on the Moon in 1971 as the commander of *Apollo 14*. Clearly, Bezos was paying homage to some of his heroes.

Stone approached Bezos during the writing of the article and asked for confirmation of some of the details. He also asked the question whether Bezos was investigating private spaceflight because of a frustration with the pace of developments over at NASA. Bezos replied via his Blackberry and explained that, no, his work was in no way a comment on NASA, whose spacecraft, engineers, programmes and astronauts were the inspirational shoulders on which he stood. He was also keen to point out that this was incredibly early days for Blue Origin, and that few practical steps had been taken so far (Stone 2018: 198–9).

Wider news about Blue Origin and Bezos' involvement in spaceflight began to filter out around 2005. But by this stage, Bezos was no longer the only billionaire kid on the block who was making inroads into the world of private space exploration. Elon Musk, for example, had founded Space Exploration Technologies Corp. – trading as SpaceX – in 2002, with the long-term goal of reducing space transportation costs and an ultimate vision of travelling to Mars to begin its colonization. Richard Branson formed Virgin Galactic in 2004, also intent on developing commercial spaceflight and space tourism. Notably, Musk and Bezos actually had a meal in 2004 to discuss their space efforts and share ideas. Christian Davenport, in his book *The Space Barons: Elon Musk, Jeff Bezos, and the Quest to Colonize the Cosmos*, describes how during the meal they discussed rocket architectures, and that Musk questioned some of Bezos' technical strategies, saying that SpaceX had already tried them and they were non-starters. Musk also noted that the advice was 'largely ignored' (Davenport 2019: 55).

LAUNCH VELOCITY

It was not long before physical manifestations of the Blue Origin space programme began to take to the skies. The first airborne system was the flight test vehicle *Charon* (named after one of Pluto's moons), which was used to test and analyze autonomous guidance and control systems. Powered by four Rolls-Royce Viper jet engines, the craft – which to the untrained eye looked something like a cross between discarded scaffolding and a rocket-powered bedstead – lifted off from Moses Lake, Washington on 5 March 2005, flying to a height of just 96 m (316 ft).

The next test vehicle was *Goddard*, the first development vehicle towards the *New Shepard*. *Goddard* lifted off for the first time on 13 November 2006 at Launch Site One, climbing for approximately ten seconds to 85 m (279 ft), then descending vertically to make a controlled vertical landing back on its landing legs. Shortly after, Bezos went openly public about the Blue Origin project. In a press release from the company on 2 January 2007, he explained simply:

> Our first objective is developing New Shepard, a vertical take-off, vertical-landing vehicle designed to take a small number of astronauts on a sub-orbital journey into space. On the morning of November 13, 2006, we launched and landed Goddard – a first development vehicle in the New Shepard program. The launch was both useful and fun. Many friends and family came to watch the launch and support the team.

The paragraph that followed this statement is particularly interesting, as if Bezos was recognizing that shareholders and commercial partners would be keen to see that his focus was still on Amazon, while also seeing a promotional opportunity:

> As an aside, all the images and videos on this website are served by Amazon's Simple Storage Service. S3 provides a simple web services interface that can be used to store and retrieve data from anywhere on the web. It gives any software developer access to the same scalable data storage infrastructure that Amazon uses to run its own websites. If you're interested, you can learn more at aws. amazon.com. (Yes, that was a brief sales pitch for Amazon Web Services, and now I return you to rockets.)

Bezos' plug for Amazon is in fact not at a tangent to the Blue Origin project, as Amazon's existence and growth and Bezos' personal wealth derived from the company were utterly central to his space adventure. For by the time the company started launching test vehicles, Blue Origin was a major enterprise, replete with staff, R&D budgets, hi-tech manufacturing, software development, and myriad other escalating costs. By May 2014, Blue Origin had 450 employees – four years later that number would balloon to 2,000. Bezos was essentially funding Blue Origin himself, largely through sales of his personal stock. By July 2014, Bezos had sunk more than $500 million of his own fortune into Blue Origin, and by 2017 he was spending $1 billion per year on space.

But there was much work to do and much to think about, so every dollar would be needed. Major investment and innovation were sunk particularly into engine design, as Bezos was looking to develop a new breed of cost-effective powerplant. A key moment in the programme was achieved on 29 April 2015, when *New*

Shepard made its first suborbital development test flight, rising to an altitude of 93.5 km (307,000 ft). The mission was largely a success, although the propulsion module was lost during the descent – to fulfil the mission of a completely reusable spacecraft, everything had to come back to Earth safely, and require minimal turnaround time before it could be launched again. The second launch came on 23 November the same year, and Bezos' ebullience at the launch results couldn't be more evident in the press release:

> 'Now safely tucked away at our launch site in West Texas is the rarest of beasts—a used rocket,' said Jeff Bezos, founder of Blue Origin. 'Blue Origin's reusable New Shepard space vehicle flew a flawless mission—soaring to 329,839 feet and then returning through 119-mph high-altitude crosswinds to make a gentle, controlled landing just four and a half feet from the center of the pad. Full reuse is a game changer, and we can't wait to fuel up and fly again.'

The New Shepard *booster, fully demonstrating Bezos' focus on reusability in spaceflight, lands in the West Texas desert after a successful mission to space on 2 May 2019.*

He would not have to wait long. Multiple further successful test launches were made – three alone in 2016.

Fifteen test flights after the programme began, in July 2021 the*New Shepard* spacecraft took its first passengers into space, and among them was Jeff Bezos himself. It was a momentous moment for both the man and for the space programme that he had created. But this was by no means the culminating point of Blue Origin – two more crewed *New Shepard* missions were flown

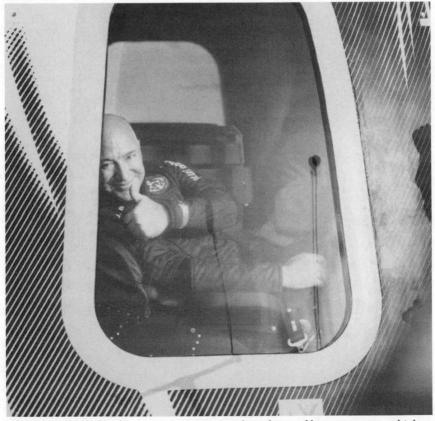

Clearly enthralled by his journey into space aboard one of his own space vehicles, astronaut Jeff Bezos gives the 'thumbs up' after returning to Earth on 20 July 2021.

by the end of the year. One of them, on 13 October, had among its four-person crew a distinctive passenger – the actor William Shatner, who was for Bezos, and an entire generation of people in their middle years, the true face of the *Star Trek* franchise, Captain James T. Kirk of the spaceship USS *Enterprise*. Shatner himself remarked on being chosen for the mission: 'I've heard about space for a long time now. I'm taking the opportunity to see it for myself. What a miracle.' Shatner also gave Blue Origin another first – at 90 years old, he is the oldest person to date to go into space. Also on board were: Blue's Origin's vice president of Mission & Flight Operations, Audrey Powers, who was an engineer, pilot and former NASA flight controller; Glen de Vries, the chief executive and co-founder of Medidata Solutions, a clinical trial software company, and vice chair Life Sciences and Healthcare at Dassault Systèmes; and Chris Boshuizen, the co-founder of Earth-imaging company Planet. Note that both de Vries and Boshuizen had paid to take their seats aboard *New Shepard*. (Tragically, de Vries was killed in a light aircraft crash four weeks after his journey into space.) Indeed, the Blue Origin press release about the NS-18 mission referred to de Vries and Boshuizen as 'our two customers'. Blue Origin was clearly demonstrating that regular commercial spaceflight was a realizable ambition, not least because *New Shepard* was showing that everyday citizens could go into space simply as paying customers. Traditionally, the only people destined to go into space were an elite of an elite, mostly former military aviators and space scientists who had managed to pass the exacting years of training to qualify them as astronauts. Bezos was, yet again, breaking moulds and conventions and placing the customer centre stage in his thinking.

GOING FURTHER

At the time of writing, in the early months of 2022, the next major step in the Blue Origin programme is the launch of the first *New Glenn* reusable launch vehicle, scheduled for late 2022. While *New Shepard* has now regularly demonstrated sub-orbital flight, it is actually just the first incremental step in a broadening scheme of development aiming to go well beyond Earth into deeper space. Named after the NASA astronaut John Glenn, *New Glenn* is a heavy-lift orbital launch vehicle, development of which began in 2012. As a generic type, a launch vehicle is a spacecraft designed to lift a payload (e.g. other spacecraft, robotic rovers, landers, satellites, scientific equipment) out to Earth orbit or beyond, and they are classified according to their low-Earth orbit payload capability – small-lift, medium-lift, heavy-lift and super-heavy lift. One in the heavy-lift category is able to transport a payload of 20,000–50,000 kg (44,000–110,000 lb). It is a two-stage rocket, 98 m (322 ft) in height and 7 m (23 ft) in diameter.

Like *New Shepard*, *New Glenn* has been built with reusability as a core requirement. The first stage, fitted with seven throttleable BE-4 LOX/LNG engines, is designed to blast the spacecraft into orbit, whereupon the stages separate, the second stage continuing onwards to deliver the payload, before returning to Earth under the pull of the planet's gravity, burning up as it re-enters the Earth's atmosphere. The first stage, however, is being built with a reusability of at least 25 missions, something unheard of to date in the history of space exploration. It returns to Earth in much the same way as *New Shepard*, but on water: its first stage makes an autonomously controlled vertical landing on the flat deck of a large recovery ship.

Logically, *New Glenn* is an evolution in Bezos' long-term ambition to erect colonies in space – to do so requires requires a launch vehicle capable of taking people and payloads into space on a regular basis. But *New Glenn* is also a potential expression of Bezos' ultra-competitive commercial sensibilities – after all, space is rapidly becoming the emerging market of the future. The Blue Origin publicity regarding *New Glenn* focuses on its applications to 'civil, commercial and national security customers', with a particular emphasis on the fact that the system offers cost-effectiveness combined with 'high availability'. The cost savings to the high-end clients come from the size of the payload offered by the 7m (23ft) diameter fairing, which Blue Origin states has 'two times the payload of any existing launch vehicle', meaning that customers can achieve, in retail terms, better returns on costs through volume outputs. The promise of high availability, furthermore, is based on both the proclaimed reliability of the system, with the promise of being 'able to launch and land in 95% of weather conditions', but also on the basis that its reusable model means a fast turnaround time between missions, the company looking to establish a cadence of eight missions a year.

Cost savings, reliability and speed – all principles Bezos used to underpin Amazon. Blue Origin has, furthermore, already won customers on this basis. The principal ones are from the commercial communications satellite sector. By 2019, Eutelsat, mu Space Corp, SKY Perfect JSAT Group, OneWeb and Telesat had all signed contracts with Blue Origin for satellite launch services; several of them committed to multi-launch agreements.

As we have seen repeatedly throughout this book, Bezos orientates towards ways that upset traditional pricing and service models for any sector he enters, and payload launches into space are no exception. One of the most significant offers was announced in July 2018 by Ted McFarland, Blue Origin's former commercial director. He stated that *New Glenn's* first five missions will each carry the payload of a solo customer, but from flight six the spacecraft will allow a 'dual-manifesting capability' – i.e. the payloads of two customers can be carried in the same mission, resulting in cost reductions for each of the customers by splitting the price of the launch between them. And in a further iteration of the customer-focused philosophy, MacFarland explained that if the schedule for one of the payload customers slipped beyond the launch date, then Blue Origin would still go ahead with the scheduled launch for the other customer on the agreed day, with no increase in cost. *New Glenn* was designed from the outset as a competitive option in satellite launch, specifically looking to outperform in both volume and flexibility the other main vehicles for satellite deployment – Arianespace's *Ariane 5*, International Launch Services' *Proton* and SpaceX's *Falcon 9*. Bezos is fully prepared to weather short-term losses if that means the customer is always well served and content.

DISPUTES

Beyond the commercial sector, Blue Origin has also been in the bidding for government agreements. Here, Bezos found himself in a direct competitive environment with the man who (according to Davenport, mentioned on page 132) gave him negative advice about his spaceflight programme back in 2004, Elon Musk, founder and CEO of SpaceX. SpaceX is a peer competitor, ideologically as well as commercially, of Blue Origin in many of its core markets, and the contract bidding process has on occasion degenerated into serious dispute. The first major government contract secured by Blue Origin came in 2018, with the announcement that the company had won a Launch Services Agreement (LSA) partnership with the US Air Force to utilize *New Glenn* for National Security Space (NSS) missions. The contract was actually one of three awarded to develop launch system prototypes, going to Northrop Grumman Innovation Systems and United Launch Alliance as well as Blue Origin. The total value of all the contracts was $2 billion, with $500 million of that going to Blue Origin – Bezos was now no longer funding the Blue Origin effort entirely from his own purse. In an article by Sandra Erwin for SpaceNews.com ('Air Force awards launch vehicle development contracts to Blue Origin, Northrop Grumman, ULA'; 10 October 2018), Erwin noted that 'SpaceX previously received an LSA award but did not make the cut this time. However, SpaceX remains eligible to bid on future Air Force launch contracts, Pentagon officials said.' Erwin did point out that the Air Force could not actually confirm whether SpaceX was in the bidding or not, but given its previous involvement in Air Force bids, in all likelihood it was.

Yet when it comes to bidding wars, not everything has led to victory for Bezos. In April 2020, Blue Origin was awarded $579 million from NASA to begin work on the development of lunar landers as part of NASA's Artemis programme, which runs with the aim of putting astronauts back on the surface of the Moon by 2024. The work was part of the Human Landing System (HLS), a sub-programme within Artemis, and Blue Origin wasn't the only player here – NASA actually issued three contracts for HLS, the two others going to SpaceX ($135 million) and Dynetics

($253 million). Furthermore, Blue Origin was head of a 'National Team' of partners, which included Lockheed Martin, Northrop Grumman, and Draper, plus 200 other small- and medium-sized suppliers across 47 US states. Going by the company's press release, Blue Origin clearly saw itself in a strong position: 'Together, these partners guided Apollo, established routine orbit cargo transfer, developed today's only crewed lunar spaceship, and pioneered planetary precision landing with liquid hydrogen/liquid oxygen vehicles. The proposed solution uses flight heritage and modularity to manage risk, move fast, and attain sustainable operations on the Moon.' Yet on 16 April 2021, NASA announced that the future work on the lander had been awarded in full to SpaceX.

The NASA decision triggered a near-immediate fightback from Bezos and Blue Origin, and on 26 April Blue Origin filed a protest with the Government Accountability Office (GAO). On 26 July, Bezos then posted a lengthy open letter to Bill Nelson, the NASA administrator. He opened the letter by stating the reliability inherent in the Blue Origin approach to the HLS, citing factors such as the sustainability and flexibility of their risk-reduced design. He then arrived at the heart of his complaints:

> Yet, in spite of these benefits and at the last minute, the Source Selection Official veered from the Agency's oft-stated procurement strategy. Instead of investing in two competing lunar landers as originally intended, the Agency chose to confer a multi-year, multi-billion-dollar head start to SpaceX. That decision broke the mold of NASA's successful commercial space programs by putting an end to meaningful competition for years to come. It also eliminated the benefits of utilizing the broad and capable supply

base of the National Team (as opposed to funding the vertically-integrated SpaceX approach) and locks every trip to the Moon into 10+ Super Heavy/Starship launches just to get a single lander to the surface. By the Agency's own admission, it bets our return to the Moon on a single solution of 'immense complexity and heightened risk associated with the very high number of events necessary to execute the front end [with] risk of operational schedule delays.'

Instead of this single source approach, NASA should embrace its original strategy of competition. Competition will prevent any single source from having insurmountable leverage over NASA. Without competition, a short time into the contract, NASA will find itself with limited options as it attempts to negotiate missed deadlines, design changes, and cost overruns. Without competition, NASA's short-term and long-term lunar ambitions will be delayed, will ultimately cost more, and won't serve the national interest.

The second paragraph takes us into the heart of Bezos' worldview. In the history of spaceflight since the end of the Second World War in 1945 until the rise of the 'space barons' in the early 2000s, the primary strata of competition existed between competing nations, especially that between the superpowers of the United States and the Soviet Union during the Cold War. Within the United States and the USSR, however, there was no real internal competition, just the drive to hit benchmarks and deadlines in relation to the overseas pressure. But in the new environment of commercial space exploration and spaceflight provision, Bezos sees competition as the optimal condition for driving dynamic and rapid innovation, and to resist the pressures of slipping back into ossified inefficiency and poor value for money. Although Bezos and Amazon have been accused of establishing monopolies in some market areas, for Bezos, the domination of a market is the product of excelling in a competitive field, and then maintaining a competitive edge to prevent the internal complacency that allows nippy competitors to emerge later and take the lead.

Bezos provided some more concrete objections to the SpaceX award, alleging that only SpaceX was given the opportunity to revise its price and funding structure, which Blue Origin was not. In more conciliatory mode, he also made several offers of generous innovation to bring Blue Origin back into the fold, including:

- Bridging the HLS budgetary funding shortfall by 'waiving all payments in the current and next two government fiscal years up to $2B to get the program back on track right now'.
- Developing and launching a pathfinder mission to low-Earth orbit of the lunar descent element, at Blue Origin's own cost.
- Taking a fixed-priced contract for the work, thereby protecting NASA from project overrun costs.

It was a hard-working letter, and the tone and content make clear the depth of Bezos' personal incredulity at the nature of the NASA decision. But in November 2021, NASA was told that the US Court of Federal Claims had rejected Blue Origin's bid protest, and thus NASA should recommence its work with SpaceX to fulfil the HLS programme. As if cognizant of Bezos' objections about NASA producing a non-competitive environment, the NASA press release of 4 November added that, 'In addition to this contract, NASA continues working with multiple American companies to bolster competition and commercial readiness for crewed transportation to the lunar surface. There will be forthcoming opportunities for companies to partner with NASA in establishing a long-term human presence at the Moon under the agency's Artemis program, including a call in 2022 to U.S. industry for recurring crewed lunar landing services.'

Given the sheer effort and cost of attempting to build his own space programme, it is worth a pause at this juncture to reflect more deeply on why Bezos was in space (literally), and the space business, in the first place.

LOOKING UP

Bezos' decision to invest his time, money and energy in developing a private space programme can appear almost hubristic, the stuff of nations not of ambitious individuals, no matter how wealthy they are. But scanning back across Bezos' life to date, a fixation on space and spaceflight is far more enduring than his later commercial visions. He was particularly inspired when, as a five-year-old, he watched the *Apollo 11* Moon landing in grainy black-and-white on his TV. He later would recall the excitement tingling in the room, the sense that history was being made and that they were privileged to watch it. All things *Star Trek* permeated his boyhood leisure hours, and he became an avid reader of science fiction, digesting dozens of volumes in a local library during his summer holidays. Science and technology, which took a tenacious grip in Bezos' thinking as he advanced through his childhood and adolescence, had a natural synergy with space exploration and astronomy. At high school, he wrote an essay entitled 'The Effect of Zero Gravity on the Aging Rate of the Common Housefly'; it was of sufficient quality to win him a visit to the NASA Marshall

Space Flight Center in Huntsville, Alabama. We remember also his high-school valedictorian speech on 20 June 1982, in which Bezos publicly outlined his belief that the future lay in vast space colonies circling the Earth, turning our planet into a 'huge national park'. One of Bezos' earliest career ambitions was to be an astronaut.

During the 1980s, a key source of inspiration for Bezos – one that continues to inspire him to this day – was the future-looking intuitions of Princeton physics professor Gerard O'Neill. In the 1970s, O'Neill had risen to public prominence for his ideas about the practical steps for creating viable space colonies and why we should do so. His salient point was not that we should focus on building such colonies on planets, but rather in space itself. Bezos was at Princeton at the time when O'Neill was teaching there, and he attended some of O'Neill's seminars. What he heard there would put down some formative roots for Bezos' future space ambitions. As noted previously, Bezos also became the president of the Students for the Exploration and Development of Space (SEDS) society.

A compelling interest in space is not uncommon in young people and indeed many adults, but for the vast majority it tends to stay in the realm of intellectual interest, while a lucky few might make a career in space-related industries. An elite minority even jump through countless performance hoops to become astronauts. Bezos' perennial fascination with space, however, has fortuitously aligned with the exceptional financial means at his disposal. But it is slipshod to present Bezos as simply a bored billionaire with too much time and money on his hands, exploring space simply as a curiosity. Nothing could be further from the truth. Bezos is deadly serious about his space work, as Mark Bezos, Jeff's brother, stated in an interview with Jeff in 2017:

'You've been passionate about space your whole life, but this is not just a plaything for you.' Bezos replied earnestly, 'No. God. No.' The heart of his conviction was expressed in the opening sentences to a speech Jeff gave on 9 May 2019 in Washington DC, at the unveiling event for Blue Origin: 'Blue Origin is the most important work I'm doing. I have a great conviction about it, based on a simple argument: Earth is the best planet.' Understanding what Bezos means by this is not just a window into his views on space, but also into the way the man looks at the physical world around him and his place within it.

'Earth is the best planet' is a statement Bezos offers at face value. While many science-fiction writers and some space scientists have contemplated the possibility of mass colonies on other planets, for Bezos this is something of a non-starter, given the hostility of the environments out there. Even the most comparatively benign of the planets in our solar system, Mars, is by its very nature utterly hostile to human life. Bezos does see a purpose, a critical one, for other planets (we shall return to it promptly), but when it comes to amenable conditions for general living, the planets just aren't credible. (Elon Musk, with his efforts towards Mars missions, may be the counterweight to this argument.) But as Bezos explained, Earth has a critical problem – its resources are finite. He has described the mathematical inevitability that we will run out of energy sources, based on a 3 per cent compounding planetary energy usage every year, *despite* incredible advances in the efficiency of appliances and energy generation. In fact, Bezos points out that the repeated leaps we have taken in energy efficiency can be part of the problem, because cheap energy dramatically encourages the proliferating use of energy-consuming appliances, industries and lifestyles, which in turn accelerates the overall energy debit. Nor is renewable energy the answer – Bezos offers the insight that in 200 years' time, at the current rate of energy compounding, we would have to cover the entire Earth in solar panels to generate enough power. The fact is that if nothing changes, the future of the planet lies in the collapse of energy sources and heavy rationing.

'So what can we do?' asked Bezos in his speech in 2019. His answer, connecting with the earlier visions of O'Neill, 'If we build this vision, these O'Neill Colonies, where does it take us? What does it mean for Earth? Earth ends up zoned residential and light industry. It'll be a beautiful place to live. It'll be a beautiful place to visit. It will be a beautiful place to go to college and to do some light industry. But ... all the polluting industry, all the things that are damaging our planet, those will be done off earth. We get to preserve this unique gem of a planet, which is completely irreplaceable.' The two gates leading to this vision he noted are; a radical reduction in launch cost and using in-space resources.

Bezos quickly followed up by saying that it was impossible to tell whether these colonies would ever be built, and admitted that he was likely not going to be the one to do so, given the generations of time it will take for such plans to come to fruition technologically. But fending off potential detractors, he explained that it was crucial for the work to begin *now*, such was its long-term importance. The human tendency to focus on short-term outcomes at the expense of long-term emergencies had to be counteracted, and here is where Bezos could play his part.

Another significant window into Bezos' thinking was the company motto of Blue Origin, '*Gradatim Ferociter*', which managed to convey both patience and urgency in one beautiful encapsulation: 'Step by Step, Ferociously'. Evidently, Bezos sees Blue Origin in very different development terms to the breakneck pace of his commercial expansion. Blue Origin's current mission statement expresses this:

> We are not in a race, and there will be many players in this human endeavor to go to space to benefit Earth. Blue's part in this journey is building a road to space with our reusable launch vehicles, so our children can build the future. We will go about this step by step because it is an illusion that skipping steps gets us there faster. Slow is smooth, and smooth is fast.

Note that the last sentence of this statement is an inspired borrowing from US Navy SEAL training programmes. Unlike Bezos' development of Amazon, which is replete with impetuous and failed ventures, executed at almost unsustainable pace, it is clear that the stakes of space exploration have produced a more considered and sustainable vision. The incrementalism inherent in the Blue Origin programme was also clarified by Bezos in the press conference after his first space flight in 2021, during which he related what he was doing with how he constructed Amazon:

> I know what that feels like. I did it three decades ago, almost three decades ago, with Amazon. Big things start small. But you can tell, you can tell when you're onto something and this is important. We're going to build a road to space so that our kids and their kids can build the future. We need to do that. We need to do that to solve the problems here on Earth. This is not about escaping

Earth. Every time I read an article about people wanting to escape Earth, no, no, no, no, no. The whole point is this is the only good planet in this solar system.

Given the absolute disparity between space exploration and running an e-commerce and digital services company, it might appear disconnected for Bezos to link his experience of starting Amazon with that of starting Blue Origin. But one of the more revolutionary aspects of the recent emergence of the space barons is the application of entrepreneurial business models to what was previously a fairly siloed scientific and engineering field. In his 2019 address, Bezos explains his thinking about both the type of spacecraft Blue Origin is designing and the transformations that

Jeff Bezos poses alongside the founding members of Blue Origin's Club for the Future foundation on 9 May 2019. The mission of the foundation is 'to inspire future generations to pursue careers in STEM and to help invent the future of life in space'.

those changes can bring to space exploration. The reusability function of *New Shepard* and *New Glenn*, for example, means that the spacecraft can be flown more regularly with minimal refurbishment between flights. More regular flights mean more experience on the part of both astronauts and engineers, and the ability to fly more people and cargo. More experience translates to more efficiency and improved safety, two progressions that also equate with cost savings for both the operator and the paying customer. All these improvements mean that space travel becomes 'routine', no longer a sequence of relatively rare and exceptional events with much downtime in between.

Here, we can again pick out the 'virtuous flywheel' principle we saw Bezos apply so aggressively to Amazon, translated across to another domain, the cyclical movement between service improvements and customer experience gathering energy and scale over time. Bezos likens the process to choosing a surgeon for an operation – you want a surgeon who has been practising and improving his craft on a regular basis week in and week out, not someone who only occasionally conducts an operation followed by a long period of inactivity.

Another element of Bezos' approach to spaceflight, as in Amazon, is technological innovation as a force for change, breaking moulds and providing new ways of exposing opportunities. One aspect he highlighted in the 2019 speech, for example, was Blue Origin's innovations in engine propellants, especially the use of liquid hydrogen, 'the highest-performing rocket fuel but also the most difficult to work with'. The first liquid-hydrogen engine developed in the *New Shepard* programme was the BE-3, which produces an impressive thrust of 490 kN (110,000 lbf) at full power but can be throttled down to just 110 kN (25,000 lbf) to enable *New Shepard* to make controlled vertical landings. The first key milestone in the development of the BE-3 was announced in 2013, but other engines for different operational parameters and spacecraft have gone into the works at Blue Origin. The BE-4 is a more powerful liquid oxygen/liquefied natural gas (LNG) rocket that Blue Origin is building for its *New Glenn* rocket as well as United Launch Alliance's (ULA) Vulcan Centaur two-stage-to-orbit heavy lift vehicle. (At the time of writing, the BE-4 is three years behind schedule.) There is also the BE-7, an engine under development for use in Blue Origin's lunar lander Blue Moon. The technicalities of each of the engine types is not our concern here, but the use of liquefied natural gas in the engines is important to Bezos not just for performance but also in terms of cost: 'Liquefied natural gas is very inexpensive. Even though there are millions of pounds of propellant on *New Glenn*, the cost of fuel and oxidizer is less than $1 million—insignificant in the scheme of things.' Bezos recognizes that for Blue Origin, the management of costs is not a peripheral consideration, even in an environment that deals in the billions of dollars. Instead, strict and scalable cost modelling is at the heart of the viability of future space flight.

One of the final points Bezos made in his address was the issue of where to find 'in-space resources', the raw materials and locations that can be used to fuel, build and supply the space colonies of the future. The answer for Bezos is the largest object seen in the night sky from Earth – the Moon. The Moon, he explains, has water trapped in ice in the craters around the poles, and by using electrolysis, the water from the ice can be transformed into hydrogen and oxygen, and there we have two elements capable of being used as spacecraft propellant. The Moon also offers considerable convenience in terms of location and operational physics. It is just three days away from Earth, meaning that launches to the Moon could take place with almost mundane frequency. (In perhaps a dig at Musk's focus, he also pointed out that there-and-back missions to Mars would require intervals of 26 months between launches.) The Moon has a gravity six times less than that experienced on Earth, which has two key plus points – first, it facilitates the easier manipulation of very heavy objects in construction projects, and second, it requires far less energy to lift objects from the face of the Moon that it does from Earth.

To make working on the Moon viable, however, Bezos recognized that 'the moon also needs infrastructure'. At the May 2019 speech, therefore, Bezos proudly displayed a Blue Moon lunar lander, which will have cargo and human payload versions. The Blue Moon website predicts that the lander system will 'enable a sustained human presence on the Moon'. This vision comes directly from Bezos' belief that 'It's time to go back to the Moon, this time to stay.' As we noted earlier in this chapter, for Bezos Earth is no longer enough.

WHERE NEXT?

Chiming with his views on the importance of future space colonies, on 25 October 2021, Blue Origin issued a press release announcing that Blue Origin and Sierra Space – a Colorado-based space company whose website strapline is 'Giving humanity a platform in space' – would develop Orbital Reef, a commercially developed, owned and operated space station in low-Earth orbit. The description of the intended space station resonates closely with the ideals of offshore living sketched by O'Neill and embraced by Bezos, while also strictly toeing the Bezos line on cost, efficiency and value for the customer. The space station is seen in terms of a 'mixed use business park in space', one that 'will offer research, industrial, international, and commercial customers the cost-competitive end-to-end services they need, including space transportation and logistics, space habitation, equipment accommodation, and operations including onboard crew'. The station has a modular design, allowing for its expansion with additional customer units, an architecture which means that the facilities of the space station grow with market demand – again the flywheel is spinning here.

As the press release noted, Orbital Reef is not an exclusive Blue Origin project. Blue Origin's main responsibilities are utility systems, large-diameter core modules and the reusable heavy-lift launch system (*New Glenn*) to transit to and from the space station. Partner Sierra Space will provide Large Integrated Flexible Environment (LIFE) modules, node modules, and the runway-landing Dream Chaser spaceplane for crew and cargo transportation. Beyond Sierra Space, other team members on the project include Boeing, Redwire Space, Genesis Engineering Solutions and Arizona State University. Boeing will also support flights between the Earth and the space station with their Starliner vehicle, and Genesis Engineering Solutions will provide the Single Person Spacecraft for operations outside the space station. NASA is feeding into the project, with Blue Origin receiving $130 million specifically for use in the development of Orbital Reef; with the International Space Station (ISS) reaching the end of its viable operational life, it is likely that Orbital Reef will be its replacement – the Orbital Reef consortia predict that it will become operational in the second half of the 2020s.

An interesting aside to Bezos' work with Blue Origin is that of Amazon's 'Project Kuiper'. Project Kuiper was announced in 2019 when Bezos still had a firm hand on Amazon's rudder. It is an ambitious programme to launch a mammoth number of communication satellites (reportedly 3,236) into orbit, surrounding the planet at an altitude of between 590 and 630 km (370 and 390 miles). Their purpose is to provide 'low-latency, high-speed broadband connectivity to unserved and underserved communities around the world'. Kuiper demonstrates one element of the ongoing competition between Bezos and Musk, with an initial investment of more than $10 billion in Kuiper. In June 2019, Bezos was interviewed by Jenny Freshwater, leader of forecasting and capacity planning at Amazon, during Amazon's inaugural re:MARS conference in Las Vegas, a forum for discussing various topics relating to technology and space (MARS stands for Machine learning, Automation, Robotics and Space). Bezos outlined, with a typically out-the-ballpark sense of the possibilities, for 'servicing the whole world' with access to broadband internet, which he also described as very close to being a 'fundamental human need' for all the citizens of a future Earth. The interview was temporarily interrupted by the intervention of an animal rights protestor, who managed to make it on to the stage before being rapidly whisked off by the security team. After this, however, Freshwater asked a perceptive question about whether Amazon might one day have FCs on the Moon. Bezos admitted that he hadn't given that possibility any thought – it is perfectly reasonable to think that he has contemplated this since.

RECOVERING HISTORY

It is easy to slip into the impression that Bezos' gaze is always firmly glued on future horizons, letting the past bury itself and forging ahead with innovation and advancement at all costs. But this is not to say that Bezos has no interest in past glories and achievements, and when it comes to spaceflight in particular, he has a considerable respect for the Herculean efforts to struggle beyond our own planet. When he speaks of the seminal leaps and epic spaceflights of NASA, there is often an awed reverence in his voice and writings. He recognizes that in relation to his own foray into space exploration, he truly stands on the shoulders of the giants who preceded him. Such is evident in the naming of this spacecraft.

As we have seen, the *Apollo 11* 1969 Moon landing still reaches out to him from his childhood, a nostalgia that coalesced into an ambitious idea one day in 2012, while he was sitting in his living room. On 28 March that year, Bezos posted a blog entry on the website of Bezos Expeditions – Bezos' personal investment company and a vehicle for pursuing his personal interests (covered more in the next chapter) – in which he outlined how the experience of his five-year-old self would inspire his first foray into underwater archaeology:

> Millions of people were inspired by the Apollo Program. I was five years old when I watched *Apollo 11* unfold on television, and without any doubt it was a big contributor to my passions for science, engineering, and exploration. A year or so ago, I started to wonder, with the right team of undersea pros, could we find and potentially recover the F-1 engines that started mankind's mission to the moon?

The *Apollo 11* mission blasted off from Kennedy Space Center on Merritt Island, Florida, on 16 July at 13.32 UTC (Coordinated Universal Time), beginning its 384,400 km (238,861-mile) journey between Earth and the Moon. 'Blasted' is an operative word here. *Apollo 11* ripped beyond Earth's atmosphere via a three-stage Saturn V rocket, at launch standing taller than the Statue of Liberty and weighing 2.8 million kg (6.2 million lb), the weight of about 400 elephants. The power to lift this monster and accelerate it came from five giant Rocketdyne F-1 engines, which together generated 34.5 million N (7.6 million lb) of thrust at launch, each of the five engines gobbling up 2,578 kg (5,683 lb) of oxidizer and fuel. After just 30 seconds from static position, the entire monumental craft had reached a speed of 1,102 km/h (685 mph), but by the time it was pushing into orbit it was travelling at more than 11.25 km (7 miles) per second. At an altitude of about 61 km (38 miles), some 88.5 km (55 miles) downrange from Cape Kennedy, however, the first stage of the *Apollo 11* spacecraft separated and the mighty F-1 engines returned to Earth, splashing down as intended in the Atlantic Ocean and sinking into the black depths of the water until they came to rest 4,270 m (14,000 ft) below the surface. There was no follow-up intention of recovering these engines, until Bezos came along, more than 40 years later.

If there were any piece of historical technology that deserved our reverence it was the F-1 engine. In his blog article, Bezos explained how his initial thought about recovering the *Apollo 11* engines was motivated by the passing of time – the engines would be steadily rotting away under the corrosive effects of salt water and would one day be lost forever. He quickly went to his computer to research the location of the engines, afterwards noting that it took him no more than 15 minutes on the internet to find the radar-tracked co-ordinates of where the booster stage of *Apollo 11* had splashed down. His initial reaction was one of optimism, feeling that it was going to be a relatively straightforward recovery for a team with the means, money and will. 'I underestimated the degree of difficulty,' he confessed.

The next posting on Bezos' blog came some time later, on 20 March 2013. The opening paragraph was ebullient, the man clearly energized by what had happened:

> What an incredible adventure. We are right now onboard the Seabed Worker headed back to Cape Canaveral after finishing three weeks at sea, working almost 3 miles below the surface. We found so much. We've seen an underwater wonderland – an incredible sculpture garden of twisted F-1 engines that tells the story of a fiery and violent end, one that serves testament to the Apollo program. We photographed many beautiful objects in situ and have now recovered many prime pieces. Each piece we bring on deck conjures for me the thousands of engineers who worked together back then to do what for all time had been thought surely impossible.

Altogether, the recovery team brought up enough pieces from the bottom of the Atlantic to reconstruct two F-1 rockets, at least good enough for the purposes of display. The process had been a deep investment, the team using underwater remotely operated vehicles (ROVs) to make long, repeated trips into the absolute darkness to bring back the components one at a time, attempting to identify twisted, corroded parts with sonar and lights, raise them to the surface, and lift them tentatively aboard the vessel by crane.

Over the following months, a team from the Kansas Cosmosphere and Space Center began the sensitive labour of performing conservation on the pieces and trying to identify them. A significant problem lay in pinpointing the actual mission to which the engines belonged. Multiple Apollo programme engines had been deposited in the Atlantic, not just those of *Apollo 11*, and the combination of the heat of the original use and the decades of underwater corrosion had removed most of the component serial numbers. Finally, one of the conservators managed to draw out the faded number '2044' on one of the thrust chambers; this correlated with NASA number 6044, which is the serial number for F-1 Engine #5 from *Apollo 11*.

The engine recovered by the F-1 Engine Recovery team arrived for display at the Museum of Flight in Seattle on 16 December 2015. At the opening event, Bezos played a video showing the recovery process for an audience that included many students from Raisbeck Aviation High School, in which he connected his childhood experience with their youth, crossing temporal bridges via the F-1 engine: 'To bring those pieces up on deck and actually touch them, that brought back for me all those feelings I had when I was 5 years old and watched those missions go to the moon. If this results in one young explorer, one young adventurer, one young inventor, doing something amazing that helps the world, I'm totally fulfilled.'

CHAPTER 7
EXPANDING HORIZONS

At the time of writing, Bezos is 58 years old. At this point in life, many successful business executives and entrepreneurs find their energy beginning to soften, as they tip downwards the nose of the aircraft they have piloted for so long, making the long descent towards retirement, succession or corporate sale. Bezos is not such a creature. By contrast, his internal flywheel still seems to be spinning at a constant high rate of knots, investing, exploring and diversifying. Looking across his life, much of his appetite for new ventures seems propelled by unbroken intellectual interest, his mind searching for new information, ideas and ways to solve problems. As with many entrepreneurs, he has a low boredom threshold.

In this chapter, we explore where Bezos' interests outside Amazon have taken him. One of the biggest of these was covered in the previous chapter – Blue Origin. But as we shall see, Bezos has followed many other avenues, passions and philanthropic themes outside space exploration. Taking these pursuits into consideration helps us to develop a more rounded insight into what motivates Bezos more widely.

BEZOS EXPEDITIONS

Bezos Expeditions is an investment firm that was established in 2005 to manage Bezos' personal investment portfolio. On one level, it is a conventional investment and venture capital firm, through which Bezos pursues investments in companies that seem like good prospects or who are handling promising ideas. The drop-down menu of 'Selected Investments' on the Bezos Expeditions website (www.bezosexpeditions.com) ranges freely across companies, markets and technologies. There are some household names on the list, such as Airbnb, Twitter and Uber. Others are less prominent but are well placed for growth and relevance. They include: Basecamp, a company providing efficient remote-working capabilities; Pilot, offering book-keeping, tax and CFO (chief financial officer) services; the biotechnology firm Sana; a personalized task list app for people in their 20s called Realworld; Glassybaby, which manufactures and sells well-being craft products; and Makerbot, an engineering innovation company. All on the list are modern, interesting, and forward-thinking. As with Bezos' own career development, many of the companies he invests in are walking the high rope between take-off success and sudden failure.

Outside his investments in external companies, though, Bezos has also used Bezos Expeditions as an umbrella under which he can develop his own personal pet projects, although the phrase 'pet projects' does little justice to the scale of ambitions involved. Two of these projects – Blue Origin and the *Apollo 11* F-1 engine recovery – were recounted in the previous chapter. But there are others to be noted, not least because of their distinction from each other and because some give a sense of where Bezos sees his place in both time and the world.

THE *WASHINGTON POST*

In 2013, Bezos made a somewhat surprising addition to his portfolio of interests, when he bought the *Washington Post* newspaper for $250 million of his own money. The paper itself was iconic, but in trouble. It had been losing circulation for many years, especially among young readers, the paper struggling to adapt its revenue model and journalistic outputs to a new age of internet advertising and digital media. In Bezos' own words, later looking back on the acquisition, he originally had 'no intention of buying a newspaper' – the subsequent change of heart was 'definitely intuitive and not analysis driven'. A leading consideration, he said, was that the *Washington Post* had 'an incredibly important role to play in this democracy', and this motivated him to make the purchase. One element of the rationale is particularly arresting, the point at which Bezos reflects on the relationship between the internet and traditional media. He explained that 'There's one gift the internet brings newspapers. It destroys almost everything, but it brings one gift, and that is free global distribution.' The sense that the internet 'destroys almost everything' is interesting to hear from the mouth of a man who has been one of the leading disrupters of the internet age. At various points in the growth of the Amazon empire, we have seen Bezos deliver a meteoric level of destruction to traditional business models, the impact on the book industry being perhaps the best known. But Bezos goes on to explain the key advantage of the internet to a newspaper, which is free distribution nationally and internationally. To Bezos, it is the internet's scaling-up effect that can compensate for the loss of revenue on individual customers. He explains that the *Washington Post* had to switch its business model from one in which it made 'a lot of money per reader with a relatively small number of readers to a tiny bit of money per reader with a very large number of readers'.

Martin Baron interviews Jeff Bezos at the Washington Post *in May 2016; Bezos had acquired the famous newspaper three years previously.*

This was a classic Bezos approach, reapplied to a new market. Throughout his fostering of Amazon into a world-dominating brand, Bezos combined three mutually supportive strategies – first, build up a huge volume of customers; second, make those customers happy; third, play the long game, trusting in the fact that a mass base of content customers will eventually yield the sought-for profits. The policy seemed to work yet again at the *Washington Post*. Within three years of Bezos taking over the paper, it had doubled its web traffic, dramatically increased its online journalistic output, reconnected with a younger audience and had also moved into profit. In 2017–18, the number of digital subscriptions doubled. The paper was on the up. (To note some up-to-date figures, in 2021, the *Washington Post* had between 71 and 111 million digital unique visitors every month.)

This did not mean, however, that everyone was happy. From 2017, there was a labour dispute between *c*.880 *Washington Post* Guild members and the newspaper leadership. In an open letter in June 2018, signed by more than 400 staffers, they acknowledged some of the beneficial changes that Bezos had brought to the newspaper's commercial health, but argued for improved working conditions, benefits and pay: 'All we are asking for is fairness for each and every employee who contributed to this company's success: fair wages; fair benefits for retirement, family leave and health care; and a fair amount of job security.'

Much like Amazon's relationship to the book industry, Bezos' ownership of the *Washington Post* was to an extent almost guaranteed to produce tension and pushback from some areas of the company, as the entire business model of the company was revisited. For Bezos, growth and commercial viability are paramount. Yet at the same time, Bezos has been strict in keeping himself separate from the editorial decision-making process at the newspaper. This much is evident in that his own paper is free to print adverse reporting about their owner. On 11 October 2021, for example, the *Washington Post* published an article titled 'Inside Blue Origin: Employees say toxic, dysfunctional "bro culture" led to mistrust, low morale and delays at Jeff Bezos's space venture' – the title is evidently pulling no punches for their ultimate owner. Yet Bezos has recognized that freedom of speech for the paper is paramount if it is to fulfil the democratic role he sees for it.

Ownership of the *Washington Post* also resulted in a particularly difficult personal episode for Bezos, one that brought him into the uncomfortable spotlights of both probing media coverage and, possibly, international espionage and blackmail. The origins of the story go back to 2017, when the *Washington Post* published a series of articles by its columnist Jamal Khashoggi, a Saudi Arabian dissident journalist and general manager and editor-in-chief of Al-Arab News Channel. Khashoggi had fled Saudi Arabia in June 2017, relocating to the United States, and from September the *Washington Post* ran articles highly critical of the Saudi regime, and particularly of the crown prince of Saudi Arabia, Mohammed bin Salman. Bezos himself was acquainted with bin Salman personally. He had had dinner with the prince in April 2018, after the *Washington Post* stories were printed, and during the convivial meal they exchanged WhatsApp numbers, after which they occasionally sent each other messages. But on 1 May 2018, according to a future report by United Nations (UN) investigators: 'A message from the Crown Prince account is sent to Mr. Bezos through WhatsApp. The message is an encrypted video file. It is later established, with reasonable certainty, that the video's downloader infects Mr. Bezos' phone with malicious code.' The implications of that infection would play out later, but until that point Bezos noticed some strange effects on his phone, such as a major rise in data output.

On 2 October 2018, Khashoggi was brutally murdered in Istanbul, almost certainly within the Saudi consulate, his body dismembered and disposed of. Subsequent investigations by the CIA determined that the journalist had been killed on the direct orders of bin Salman.

After the murder of one of their own, the *Washington Post* doubled down on its adverse coverage of the Saudi regime. Then, in early 2019, came the *National Enquirer*'s breaking story about Bezos' affair with Lauren Sánchez, which contained details and images of such intimacy that Bezos ordered an investigation through the security expert Gavin de Becker. On 8 February, Bezos also published an Instagram post in which he accused American Media Inc. (AMI), the owners of the *National Enquirer*, of extortion, blackmail and acting on behalf of the Saudi government. Bezos' anger and defiance were palpable:

> Something unusual happened to me yesterday. Actually, for me it wasn't just unusual – it was a first. I was made an offer I couldn't refuse. Or at least that's what the top people at the National Enquirer thought. I'm glad they thought that, because it emboldened them to put it all in writing. Rather than capitulate to extortion and blackmail, I've decided to publish exactly what they sent me, despite the personal cost and embarrassment they threaten.

Further down the article, Bezos admits that his ownership of the *Washington Post* was 'a complexifier for me. It's unavoidable that certain powerful people who experience Washington Post news coverage will wrongly conclude I am their enemy.'

The plot soon thickened. Bezos and de Becker had Bezos' phone analyzed by digital forensic experts from FTI Consulting, who concluded with 'a medium to high confidence' that his phone had been hacked by the Saudis, giving them access to Bezos' personal messages and photos. At the same time, de Becker claimed that AMI's CEO, David Pecker, had a close relationship with bin Salman. The accusations from the Bezos camp gained further weight from a report by UN special rapporteurs Agnès Callamard and David Kaye into surveillance by the Saudi government, largely corroborating Bezos' suspicions. In a statement, Callamard and Kaye explained that, 'The information we have received suggests the possible involvement of the Crown Prince in surveillance of Mr. Bezos, in an effort to influence, if not silence, the *Washington Post*'s reporting on Saudi Arabia.'

Both AMI and the Saudi authorities pushed back. The Saudis emphatically rejected the claims of official involvement in hacking. AMI, meanwhile, stated that their principal source was none other than Lauren Sánchez's brother, Michael, and that no one else was involved as a source. Michael Sánchez, while not denying that he was a source for the story, filed a lawsuit against AMI in March 2020, claiming that he was not the 'sole source' of the story and that AMI were attempting to make him a 'scapegoat'. He alleged that AMI already had intimate information on Bezos before he spoke with the *National Enquirer* journalists.

Whatever the full picture of truth about the phone-hacking claims, the fact that the scandal played out in the full and often gleeful glare of the international media illustrates how much Bezos' public profile had changed over the years. His ownership of the *Washington Post* also brought him into conflict with, from January 2017, the incumbent US president, Donald Trump. Critical coverage of President Trump and his administration from the *Washington Post* certainly attracted the ire of the belligerent US leader, and Amazon and its boss also came into the president's line of sight, although in a tweet on 29 March 2019 he explained that his objections to Amazon predated his presidency: 'I have stated my concerns with Amazon long before the Election. Unlike others, they pay little or no taxes to state & local governments, use our Postal System as their Delivery Boy (causing tremendous loss to the

U.S.), and are putting many thousands of retailers out of business!' According to a *Guardian* article of 7 April 2018, Trump had also made suggestions that the *Washington Post* was in essence acting as a 'lobbyist' for Amazon. Any implicit connection between Bezos and the treatment of Trump in the *Washington Post* was vigorously disputed by Frederick Ryan Jr., the CEO of the newspaper, who went on to explain that Bezos had neither proposed a story to the *Washington Post* nor intervened in any editorial process. Press freedom does seem to be a core value for Bezos. In May 2017, for example, he gave $1 million to the Reporters Committee for Freedom of the Press, an organization that provides pro bono legal services for US journalists.

A further criticism of Amazon from President Trump came in April 2020, when the administration placed five of Amazon's foreign websites (Canada, UK, Germany, France and India) on its 'notorious markets' list, which it claimed were 'hotspots' for international counterfeiting and copyright infringement. Again, Amazon drove back hard, pointing out that 99.9 per cent of the Amazon pages viewed worldwide had never received complaints of counterfeiting and that the company employed some 8,000 people to combat intellectual theft.

President Trump has not been the only high-ranking political figure to level criticism at Amazon. In June 2019, for example, then presidential hopeful Joe Biden argued that despite making millions in profit, Amazon.com had not paid any federal income tax in 2018, arguing that 'we need to reward work, not wealth'. Amazon protested, explaining that it had paid $2.6 billion in corporate income tax since 2016, invested $200 billion since 2016 and created 300,000 jobs. As president, Biden also expressed sympathy for unionization efforts by Amazon workers.

We come across a regular theme in these criticisms. Much of the negative scrutiny towards Bezos is related simply to his wealth, and the disparity between that wealth and that of those who work for him or his companies. But this debate has to be discussed, as we will now, within the context of Bezos' increasingly important philanthropic and environmental interests, which together are having a profound effect in some areas of global development.

BEZOS DAY ONE FUND

In September 2018, Jeff and MacKenzie Bezos announced a new philanthropic effort, the Day One Fund. It was of sweeping scale and ambition, creating a $2 billion fund that would focus 'on making meaningful and lasting impacts in two areas: funding existing non-profits that help families experiencing homelessness, and creating a network of new, non-profit tier-one preschools in low-income communities'.

Based on the mission described, the Day One Fund bifurcates into two distinct funds: the Day 1 Families Fund and Day 1 Academies Fund. The former provides financial awards to organizations and civic groups working in the fields of providing shelter and hunger support to needy families. Looking at the statement of receiving organizations for 2021 (in which $96.2 million was awarded) for the Day 1 Families Fund, some 32 individual groups dotted across the United States received awards valued at between $750,000 and $5 million. They include Adopt-A-Family of the Palm Beaches (Lake Worth, FL, $5 million), Covenant House Alaska (Anchorage, AK, $1.25 million), Homeless Action Network of Detroit (Detroit, MI, $1.25 million), Sacramento Steps Forward (Sacramento, CA, $5 million) and Tri-County Community Action Agency, Inc. (South Boston, VA, $2.5 million).

The Bezos Day 1 Academies Fund extends the idea of assisting vulnerable communities and families by creating a network of 'Montessori-inspired' pre-schools targeted at three- to five-year-old children from low-income families. The Montessori connection is a natural one for Bezos – his own attendance at a Montessori school obviously left a favourable impression. Developed by Italian educator Maria Montessori from the early 20th century, the Montessori approach to education focuses more on giving pupils a stimulating space in which to pursue their own interests, aptitudes and activities, rather than attempting to control their mental space with a rigid teaching programme. In retrospect, this would have been an ideal learning environment for the perpetually inquisitive Bezos. In an interview for *Montessori Life* in 2000, Bezos explained how the type of education offered by Montessori was a 'very formative experience', noting the degree of stimulation the learning environment provided for his young mind. The Montessori philosophy is built into the Bezos Academy's own mission, but with the flexibility of other strategies: 'The Montessori approach allows every child to develop naturally – to learn and grow at their own pace. Our Curriculum will also borrow from other pedagogies to learn, invent, and improve our ability to support every child's development.'

The first Bezos Academy school opened for learning in Des Moines, Iowa, in October 2020. By spring 2022, the Bezos Academy had five pre-schools operating, all in Washington State, and plans to open 15 more in late 2022 and early 2023, including four in Florida, seven in Texas and four more in Washington. Why has Bezos invested so deeply in education? A clue comes from a headline on the Bezos Family Foundation website: 'How we learn shapes who we become.' We should linger over this statement a moment. Some great entrepreneurs have histories defined by their rejection or even alienation from educational systems, confirming the stirring adventurism of an individual who steps outside the system and pulls themselves up to success through dint of effort and unconventional thinking. While such narratives are inspiring, research since the 1990s tends to indicate that a prolonged and good-quality education significantly raises the possibility of entrepreneurial direction in later life. After all, even the university drop-out entrepreneur will still have received a longer period in education than most of the surrounding population. Bezos certainly seems to be a believer in the outcomes of education, particularly for children in their early years, a critical period when brain formation is actively underway and needs nourishing.

The Day One Fund efforts are not the limits of Bezos' philanthropic contributions to educational advancement, and other work has resonance with his family background. In 2013, for example, Bezos gave $500,000 to Worldreader, an organization founded by a former Amazon employee, dedicated to providing people in the developing world with free access to a library of digital books via e-readers and mobile phones, helping to foster basic literacy skills. In January 2018, Bezos announced that he and MacKenzie were donating $33 million to TheDream.US, a scholarship fund to assist young 'dreamer' immigrants in their educational advancement. In an article for the *Washington Post*, Bezos fully acknowledged the connection between his father Mike's personal journey and the donation: 'He landed in this

Jeff Bezos, at a Bezos Academy preschool, paints a mural with a student. Bezos Academy assists vulnerable communities and families through a network of tuition-free preschools that serve three- to five-year-old children from low-income families.

country alone and unable to speak English. With a lot of grit and determination – and the help of some remarkable organizations in Delaware – my dad became an outstanding citizen, and he continues to give back to the country that he feels blessed him in so many ways. MacKenzie and I are honored to be able to help today's Dreamers by funding these scholarships.'

Again, inevitably, some critics have placed question marks over his philanthropic activities. Eyebrows were raised at his not signing the Giving Pledge, a movement launched in August 2010 by Warren Buffett, Melinda French Gates and Bill Gates, in which dozens of US and international billionaires pledged to give away the majority of their wealth. Bezos was one of the only major US figures not to sign the pledge. Critics of this decision not only focused on Bezos' extreme personal wealth, but also the fact that MacKenzie, who received about $38 billion worth of Amazon stock following her divorce from Jeff (although Bezos retained voting rights over her stock), herself signed up to the Giving Pledge. Some tightened their focus more on the details of Bezos' philanthropic programmes. In a November 2018 article for Vox.com, 'Jeff Bezos's philanthropic projects aren't as generous as they seem', Gaby Del Valle argued that much of Bezos' giving through the Day One Fund was targeted at cities and states with high present or future densities of Amazon workers. She also argued that Amazon played a part in killing a Seattle city bill to tax local businesses to fund affordable housing projects and thereby counteract homelessness, although she acknowledged from an Amazon statement that the Day One Fund was Bezos' personal philanthropic effort, and not an Amazon programme.

But Del Valle raised a more interesting general argument, namely that Bezos is more a believer in the power of non-profit and private sector philanthropy than government interventions. She quotes Bezos from a Bloomberg.com article in which he explained: 'If you have a mission you can do it with government, you can do it with non-profit or for-profit. If you can figure out how to do it with for-profit that has a lot of advantages: It's self-sustaining.' While it would be too simplistic to say that Bezos sees government spending as secondary to private initiatives (his veneration for NASA's historical efforts is a counterbalance to this position, for example), his leaning towards a 'self-sustaining' model of philanthropy again reflects his long-termist thinking, as much as his declarations that his charitable giving is a focus on the short term. Private philanthropy, for example, has the potential (admittedly not always realized) to maintain itself across successive political administrations, which in democratic regimes tend to work in four- or five-year cycles, often accompanying short-termist thinking. Private money can also, again potentially, have an efficiency that government programmes, with all their multiple competing claims and political interests, can strain to match. Taking Bezos' historical actions in the round, however, we can likely say that Bezos appreciates being in control of his investments, this giving him the opportunity to apply his principles of scale, growth and maximum impact.

BEZOS AND ENVIRONMENTALISM

During an interview on stage at the 'Our Future in Space' event, Ignatius Forum, Washington National Cathedral on 11 November 2021, Bezos responded to those critics who have accused him of sinking billions of dollars into space exploration, when Earth had a far greater need of the money. He retorted that those who see an either/or relationship between space and Earth investments were missing the fact that 'we need to do both, and that the two things are deeply connected'. Indeed, it seems little understood that Bezos' investments in Earth-bound research and philanthropy actually outweigh the money he sinks into space. The more we explore these investments the more we realize that the Earth means a lot to Bezos.

As we saw in the previous chapter, Bezos' ideal for the future of space exploration and colonization is that it ultimately serves to preserve planet Earth, the undeniable jewel of the solar system, but one increasingly imperilled by the activities of just one of its 8 million species of creatures. In fact, the importance of tackling

Jeff Bezos speaks during the Climate Week NYC Leaders' Reception in 2021, where he pledged $1 billion in grants to support international conservation work.

climate change and environmental damage has been reinforced by Bezos' forays into space, as he explained during a speech to the COP26 UN climate change conference in Glasgow, United Kingdom, on 2 November 2021:

> Nature is beautiful but it is also fragile. I was reminded of this in July when I went into space with Blue Origin. I was told seeing the earth from space changes the lens through which you view the world, but I was not prepared for just how much that would be true. [. . .] Each year, forests and landscapes absorb 11 billion tons of CO_2 from the atmosphere. As we destroy nature, we reverse this process. In too many parts of the world, nature is already flipping from a carbon sink to a carbon source. This is a profound danger to us all.

By 2021, Bezos had already recognized that Amazon, and himself personally, had a part to play in the climate movement. In September 2019, Amazon announced the Climate Pledge, a commitment to reach net-zero carbon by 2040. The following year, Amazon launched The Climate Pledge Fund in 2020 to support the development of sustainable and decarbonizing technologies and services. This dedicated investment program—with an initial $2 billion in funding—invests in visionary companies whose products and solutions will facilitate the transition to a low-carbon economy. In the press launch event, Bezos explained how he wanted Amazon to be a leader in the field of sustainable energy innovations and reduced carbon emissions. He pointed to signal changes that had taken place within Amazon itself: the company running on 40 per cent renewable energy, with a commitment to 80 per cent renewable energy and net zero carbon emissions by 2040; the construction of 15 'utility scale' solar and wind farms; an investment of $440 million in Rivian, a company that produces electric delivery vans (in September 2019, Amazon placed an order for 100,000 of the vehicles). By December 2021, Amazon had invested in 274 renewable energy projects globally which, as its press release explained, could provide the power for 3 million US homes.

The Climate Pledge concept was born under Bezos, but it is an Amazon project. Bezos' uniquely personal investment in environmentalism, however, is the Bezos Earth Fund. Bezos announced the Earth Fund in February 2020. An Instagram post on 17 February explained how Bezos saw climate change as the biggest threat to the planet and humanity, and issued a rallying cry for action with the funds to back it:

Today, I'm thrilled to announce I am launching the Bezos Earth Fund. Climate change is the biggest threat to our planet. I want to work alongside others both to amplify known ways and to explore new ways of fighting the devastating impact of climate change on this planet we all share. This global initiative will fund scientists, activists, NGOs—any effort that offers a real possibility to help preserve and protect the natural world. We can save Earth. It's going to take collective action from big companies, small companies, nation states, global organizations, and individuals. I'm committing $10 billion to start and will begin issuing grants this summer. Earth is the one thing we all have in common — let's protect it, together.

– Jeff

The announcement of the fund generated much excitement in the world of environmental science, as well as some rather surprised press scrutiny in relation to Bezos' personal wealth and other projects. Journalists calculated that based on his current net worth of about $130 billion, this pledge of his own money constituted 7.7 per cent of his entire wealth. Furthermore, the financing of the Earth Fund would be greater than the money Bezos was sinking into his space programme. At the time of writing this book, $1.4 billion of funding had already been distributed. The range of project investment has been widespread, and global, and has included areas as diverse as:

- Halting deforestation and promoting sustainable land use.
- Conserving and restoring degraded landscapes.
- Investing in environmental justice efforts and communities

that have been disproportionately affected by 'disparity and pollution'.

- The development of zero-emissions ships and trucks.
- Helping Indian farmers to achieve more environmentally sustainable farming practices.
- Reducing methane pollution in the oil and gas industry.
- Decarbonization of hard-to-abate sectors, including steel, cement, and zero-emissions ships and trucks.
- Research of plant root systems to coax more carbon into the soils.
- Satellite monitoring of carbon flow and flux, and satellite monitoring of methane pollution.
- The electrification of every school bus in the United States.

Jeff Bezos, Lauren Sánchez and Colombian President Ivan Duque take in the view from Chiribiquete National Park with members of the Bezos Earth Fund and the president's team (March 2022).

The Earth Fund is undoubtedly a huge opportunity for to reverse the degradation of nature and tackle the climate crisis and seems born of Bezos' genuine concern for the planet. After all, his plans for space colonization (either in his lifetime or more likely that of future generations) only make sense if this planet is saved from climate calamity in the process – as with all Bezos' projects, there is a long-term logic to his actions. By 2030, $10 billion will have been devoted to the Earth Fund. Amazon's Climate Pledge is committed to reach net-zero carbon by 2040 (10 years ahead of the Paris Agreement), and Blue Origin's long-term vision will move heavy and polluting industries off Earth.

Jeff Bezos at the Chiribiquete National Park, in Colombia where the Bezos Earth Fund is working with partners to protect the area from deforestation.

Pulling together some of the threads regarding Bezos' philanthropic work, he made a particularly interesting comment on Twitter in 2017: 'I'm thinking about a philanthropy strategy that is the opposite of how I mostly spend my time – working on the long term. For philanthropy, I find I'm drawn to the other end of the spectrum: the right now.' For much of Bezos' life, sustaining long-term visions, regardless of short-term impacts, seems to have been a keynote of his decision-making. With his philanthropic work, however, comes the recognition that long-term social and environmental impact requires immediate intervention in the lives at those critical moments of their own development and decision. But to show that Bezos has by no means relinquished his vision of the long term, we can look at one of the more curious investments of Bezos Expeditions, the 10,000 Year Clock.

TEN THOUSAND YEARS OF TIME

The 10,000 Year Clock – also referred to as the Clock of the Long Now – is certainly something of an oddity in Bezos' portfolio. It involves the construction of a huge mechanical clock built inside a mountain in West Texas – an imposing rock slab rising 610 m (2,000 ft) above the surrounding landscape – the whole work a cross between monumental architecture and precision timepiece. The project is heroic in scale. The clock itself is hundreds of feet tall within the body of the mountain, the mechanism designed to tick away accurately across ten millennia. The chimes of the clock are programmed to play 3.5 million unique sequences, one chime sequence for every day the clock is visited over the next 10,000 years.

The clock was first conceived in the 1980s by Danny Hillis, an American inventor, entrepreneur, scientist and specialist in AI. At the time, the world was mentally attuning itself to the approaching new millennium, but Hillis wanted to break through this fleeting temporal snapshot by erecting a mechanical clock that would run for 10,000 years. Being confronted with such a clock would compel people to think about the millennia to come, their vanishing place within the grand scheme of time, but also their role to play in shaping the future by interacting beneficially with the present.

A small-scale prototype of the clock (today on display at the Science Museum in London) was up and running on 31 December 1999, just before the world ticked its way into the year 2000, but now came the matter of erecting the full-scale timepiece. The symbolism and mental focus delivered by the clock was not lost on Bezos, and Bezos Expeditions bought into funding the development.

The clock and its surroundings exert an enormous contemplative gravity, setting individual life in the context of yawning future centuries. However much Bezos focuses on the long term, he knows that time will move beyond us all.

CONCLUSION
THE BEZOS APPROACH

In the ever-expanding library dedicated to entrepreneurship, the hunt is always on for the defining qualities that bring success. As a rule, great figures of industry and innovation tend to have personalities that match the scale of their ambitions. A 2020 article for *Forbes* listed 'Six Personality Traits of Successful Entrepreneurs', which were specifically: robust work ethic; deep passion; creativity; motivated self-starters; easy-going attitude; and eager to learn. Other authorities offer alternative but generally overlapping lists (based on a web search, the number of qualities assigned to successful entrepreneurs varies between six and ten). Some add confidence, vision, flexibility, an ability to sell, strictness with money, and resilience. The key motivation behind such lists is to find a tidy set of convenient rules to success, the implication being that achievement in business is a universal recipe that can be followed by anyone.

When it comes to Jeff Bezos, however, it can be difficult to distil a set of maxims that denote the 'Bezos approach'. This is not because he does not impart some clear and useful lessons. Rather it is that the execution of those rules in Bezos' case came with an almost indefatigable capacity for work and a laser-sharp intelligence, and brutally speaking those are in many ways qualities that cannot be taught. Furthermore, Bezos seems to bring together two characteristics that in most individuals are incompatible: a deep tolerance for outrageous risk and a highly analytical desire to refine a system for maximum efficiency. When combined, the dynamic created by the marriage of these two aspects is exciting and productive, with the caution and adaptation of the latter controlling the direction and disregard of the former. Bezos, as we have seen, had more than his share of massive commercial or investment failures. But the nature of his personality and management approach means that he has constantly generated fresh opportunities, continually raising the statistical likelihood of both success and growth, and on a prodigious scale. Perhaps this is the true definition of Bezos' entrepreneurial drive – acting in a way that maximizes the possibility of success, but without the caution that comes by attempting to guarantee it.

THE CUSTOMER

So what does Bezos himself define as the root cause of his entrepreneurial big bang and subsequent expansion? We can make a solid start with one of his most famous quotations, which refers specifically to the Amazon model: 'We've had three big ideas at Amazon that we've stuck with for 18 years, and they're the reason we're successful: Put the customer first. Invent. And be patient.'

These lines of business wisdom have been mulled over by many business leaders and analysts, the words offering a mix of apparent simplicity but hidden depths. In terms of 'Put the customer first', we have seen Bezos reinforce that instinct time and time again throughout this book, not least in the case of the rise of Amazon. For Bezos, the heightened focus on customer experience is not just a buy-in to the notion that the customer is important and needs to be kept generally happy to ensure growth and repeat business. In Bezos' worldview, customers seem far more than that. They are the very engine of growth and exceeding their expectations builds the flywheel effect that he and Amazon applied to the development of the Marketplace service.

With a regularity that for Amazon executives must have been nerve-rattling, Bezos introduced a new Amazon service that, for a time, seemed to do little but erode profitability. That wouldn't make sense for a small- to medium-sized company looking to produce solid end-of-year results. But if we jump to the 'be patient' element of the Bezos quotation, we see it in its true context. Bezos never seems to have aspired to be simply a commercially successful entrepreneur, but rather a true game-changer, building a business that would somehow reshape the fundamental concepts of how business is done in an age of enabling technology. That ambition would take time, and patience, to achieve, as ultimately it was reliant upon generating an irresistible momentum via the potential energy of a huge customer base.

The single word 'Invent' defines how this is to be done. Bezos has an almost pathological resistance to anything that smacks of stasis and ossification. In a new hi-tech world replete with possibilities for innovation, an endlessly inventive attitude, backed by investment and fast-moving processes, is arguably the only way not only to stay fresh in outlook and growth, but also to protect against the throngs of newcomers who will inevitably attempt to consign your company to history or irrelevance.

LEADERSHIP

Another distinct element to Bezos' 'management style' (to employ a phrase I don't think Bezos himself would use) is his undoubted capacity to *lead*, in the fullest sense of the word. If Bezos' personal style and corporate history demonstrate one thing, it is that he is absolutely not afraid to stand alone, and generally prevail, against dissenting opinions. He is a leader who is confident to make decisions almost unilaterally and stick by them.

Note that this does not mean he acts without advice; for much of his life, Bezos has surrounded himself with truly exceptional people, allowing them to take the lead in specific areas of development and learning from them in the process. His oversight, however, is king. Many employees have also commented on or observed Bezos' probing intelligence and breadth of knowledge, which meant that whatever your position, you couldn't hide behind expertise and obfuscating language. Idi Manber, during the time he was being courted by Bezos to make the move from Yahoo to Amazon, remembered that Bezos asked him to explain a particularly complicated algorithm, one that Manber felt it would take him 'a month' to explain to most other executives. Bezos fully grasped what he was saying within the space of the meeting.

A further window into Bezos' management style can be opened through exploring some of Amazon's 'Leadership Principles', a one-page crib sheet developed during the Bezos years that explains the Amazon approach to managing operations and getting things done. There were originally 14 Leadership Principles in total, and they were actually put together by Jeff Wilke and Rick Dalzell, the CTO, but in close consultation with Bezos. As Wilke later stated in an interview, 'there's a lot of Jeff Bezos in the language'. Today, there are 16 Principles, but each of them bears the imprint and expectations of Amazon's founder. For a start, they are kept short and pithy, each a punchy heading followed by a few clipped sentences – there is nothing long-winded here, as if the document itself is striving to cull unnecessary words. In fact, they reflect what Wilke has called 'the culture of single-page communication' that Bezos preferred.

Some of the principles read as if they are describing Bezos himself:

Are Right, A Lot

Leaders are right a lot. They have strong judgment and good instincts. They seek diverse perspectives and work to disconfirm their beliefs.

Insist on the Highest Standard

Leaders have relentlessly high standards—many people may think these standards are unreasonably high. Leaders are continually raising the bar and drive their teams to deliver high quality products, services and processes. Leaders ensure that defects do not get sent down the line and that problems are fixed so they stay fixed.

Think Big

Thinking small is a self-fulfilling prophecy. Leaders create and communicate a bold direction that inspires results. They think differently and look around corners for ways to serve customers.

Dive Deep

Leaders operate at all levels, stay connected to the details, audit frequently, and are skeptical when metrics and anecdote differ. No task is beneath them.

Have Backbone; Disagree and Commit

Leaders are obligated to respectfully challenge decisions when they disagree, even when doing so is uncomfortable or exhausting. Leaders have conviction and are tenacious. They do not compromise for the sake of social cohesion. Once a decision is determined, they commit wholly.

Based on principles such as these, the ideal Amazon manager is superbly competent, with deep reserves of relevant knowledge; mentally strong and resilient; has an appetite for big visions, but the determination to manifest those visions in reality; and they are also confident enough in themselves to make or challenge decisions even if by so doing they swim against strong currents of resistance.

Bezos himself has always demonstrated an absolute, and sometimes ruthless, independence of mind, and an intolerance for ideas or arguments based on the way that things have traditionally been done. During Amazon's difficult exploration of entry into the jewellery market in the early 2000s, Bezos met with his executives to discuss the strategies of doing so. The core suggestion from his team was to let experienced jewellery sellers into Marketplace, monitor their performance and marketing strategies, and then use this information to develop Amazon's entry. Bezos thought about the strategy, then mysteriously left the room, appearing a few minutes later with a sheet of paper for each of the executives present. On the paper was printed the following sentence: 'We are the *"Unstore"'* (Stone 2018: 229). Bezos was essentially telling his leaders to stop thinking of replicating the traditional models of retail and think of Amazon as an entirely new space for innovation, free from past models.

MAKING DECISIONS

The stipulation that Amazon's leaders 'Have Backbone; Disagree and Commit' connects with Bezos' passionate views on the nature of decision-making in business and his general antipathy towards excessive levels of cross-business communication. Bezos is driven by the need to get things done in the real world, rather than gobbling up hours in merely *discussing* how to get things done. This is reflected in another of the Amazon principles:

Bias for Action
Speed matters in business. Many decisions and actions are reversible and do not need extensive study. We value calculated risk taking.

For many large businesses, this principle would appear to carry a terrifying level of risk, implying that plans would be executed without full consideration of costs and consequences. Bezos, however, is energized by risk, seeing its inherent speed as critical for building momentum and seizing the advantage. Bezos' organizational preference has therefore leaned towards small, highly intelligent teams working out problems as they arose and pushing the levels of innovation and efficiency relentlessly, without the sea anchor of constant debate and discussion holding back forward movement.

Bezos himself explained his philosophy of decision-making in an interview with RNDF, padding out the idea that 'Many decisions and actions are reversible and do not need extensive study.' Bezos divides decisions into 'one-way doors' and 'two-way doors'. A one-way-door decision is a decision that once made, cannot be reversed and that will have major consequences for the business, positive or negative. Bezos explains that these types of decisions need to be made very carefully and with a high degree of consultation, with as much data and analysis as possible brought to bear on the final decision.

The second type of decision is the two-door type. Unlike the one-door type, the two-door decision is reversible. This means that whatever the consequences, they can be undone either through retreating to the original starting position or by manoeuvring the originally intended course of events in a different direction, making adaptation for circumstances. This vision of decision-making, pioneered in Amazon and some other major tech companies, has had a pervasive effect in modern business thinking, including the now-popular 'Agile Project Management' (APM), in which iterative cycles of continuous product/service releases and subsequent customer feedback are used to push a company forwards, rather than prolonged planning and a big launch. The problem, Bezos explains, is that one-door-type decisions are quite rare, but many companies treat the far more common two-door-type solutions as one-door-type decision challenges. Thinking in this way leads to inertia and exhaustion, and a company incapable of moving at advantageous speeds.

Throughout this book, we have seen many times where Bezos steps into an arena of debate and brings it quickly to a close with a sharp executive decision. In the same interview, he explained that when company representatives are at loggerheads, attempting to win what is in essence a battle of attrition through argument, he exercises the 'disagree and commit' principle. Here, the situation is escalated to a more senior person, one who has developed, hopefully, acute powers of judgement, and who cuts through the fog and makes a decision even if the disagreements haven't been resolved. Bezos explains that, 'It's actually very calming really because it's acknowledging the reality that the senior person has a lot of judgment. That judgment is super valuable, and that's why sometimes you should overrule subordinates even when they have better ground truth. But that's your judgment.'

One particularly distinctive element of the Bezos approach is that it questions the value of communication. To be clear, Bezos doesn't want to stop employees talking together constantly in productive ways, but rather that the communication should be taking place in real time within the small teams directly involved in solving the problem in front of them, rather than escalating discussion into large and time-consuming corporate debating chambers. One of his most telling comments was delivered in response to a presentation by some junior executives in the late 1990s, who proposed a more organized dialogic approach to corporate communications. The answer must have surprised them: 'Communication is a sign of dysfunction. It means people aren't working together in a close, organic way. We should be trying to figure out a way for teams to communicate less with each other, not more' (quoted in Stone 2018: 210).

Bezos is *not* recommending slipshod, careless communication. One of Bezos' more practically striking innovations at Amazon was that he banned the use of PowerPoint or similar presentational aids when it came to running meetings, believing that the actual software format encouraged poor thinking, allowing important details to slip through the gaps in the bullet points. (Bezos is not alone in this thinking – in 2005, the US Army's Brigadier General

H.R. McMaster, then serving as a counterinsurgency advisor in the deteriorating war in Iraq, banned PowerPoint as a presentation tool in military strategy meetings, seeing it as a root cause of the mess US forces found themselves facing.) If an executive was leading a meeting, he or she would be required to write down the proposal or report in a six-page document (plus footnotes), a format in which every concept had to be properly and fully explained, with little abbreviation or padding. The document was to be given to each member of the team at the beginning of the meeting, and the first 15 minutes were spent in quiet reading, allowing people to formulate proper ideas before discussion began. This system is still in use at Amazon today.

An extension of Bezos' appetite for lean communication models is also evident in his 'two-pizza teams' idea from the early 2000s. He explained the principle as a restructuring of the company based around teams of people no larger than the number that could be fed comfortably by just two pizzas (the specific size of the pizzas was not mentioned, but we are assuming fairly large ones). This meant teams of no more than ten people, the argument being that 'the smaller the team the better the collaboration'. The two-pizza teams were not an unambiguous improvement in some departments, but they do offer further insight into the way Bezos views the flow of words and ideas within a company, and how the small-team ethos can keep the 'Day 1' start-up attitude he advocates.

We must also acknowledge that Bezos' approach to problem-solving and innovation also comes from the fact that he generally knows what he is talking about. Bezos' decisions rarely come from whim or gut instinct, but from a breadth of learning that often impresses those around him, even those ostensibly with far more experience and knowledge in a chosen field. Brad Stone relates one corporate episode at Amazon when Bruce Jones, an Amazon vice president, led five engineers over a nine-month period to develop a new algorithm to improve the movement of the pickers on the floor. After all their work and calculations, they gave a slick demonstration of what they proposed to Bezos and the S Team. At the end of their presentation Bezos, rather unimpressed, stood up and headed over to a whiteboard, where he rapidly began to map out an alternative solution. Jones remembered thinking that here was a man without any deep experience or training in operating systems management, but that everything he was writing on the board was indeed a better model for efficiency (Stone 2018: 223).

WORK-LIFE BALANCE

Bezos is undoubtedly a hard taskmaster if he is your boss. Whatever the enterprise, he has driven development with unswerving expectations of high standards, hard work and intelligent decision-making, a scrutiny that has undoubtedly produced a lot of executive casualties along the way. Despite the prestige and excitement of working for one of the most innovative companies in history, for some, the pressures of working for Bezos were simply too much.

There has been the tendency to present the Bezos work ethic as utterly dismissive of the notion of work-life balance, but delving into some of his writings upon the subject can give us a more nuanced insight into the priorities he assigns to life experience. In his article 'Recruiting Talent', he first asks the question 'Do you want mercenaries or missionaries?' Bezos classifies mercenaries as those who are basically attracted to a company because of the perks or incentives it offers, the status package. Missionaries, by contrast, are those people who are driven by an inspiring vision, a desire to pursue and achieve inspiring goals, whatever the obstacles in the way. It is easy to guess which sort of employee Bezos wants to attract.

In another RNDF interview, he squarely addressed the issue of how a human life could be constructed between the spheres of work and home/family life. For Bezos, the very term 'work-life balance' is misleading. He explains that the more people feel 'energized', interested and valued at work, the happier they will be at home. Conversely, if the employee or boss is unhappy at home, then he or she will bring that discontent to work. Bezos does not like the phrase 'work-life balance' because of its either/or sense of duality, 'it implies there's a strict trade-off'. Instead, he sees it as better to view the relationship between work and home as a flywheel or a circle, the two feeding off one another rather than being in competition.

In the same article, Bezos explains that there are two types of people in relation to the energy of a working place. He asks the readers to imagine that they are in a meeting and a person walks into the room. Either that person adds energy to the meeting, lifting the spirits and the productivity of those around him, or he deflates the mood, draining the energy from the participants. In both work and in the home, Bezos says, 'you have to decide which of those kinds of people you are going to be'. Bezos also gave one of the most revealing direct insights into his own mental operating system:

It's not about the number of hours, not primarily. I suppose if you went crazy with one hundred hours a week or something, maybe there are limits, but I've never had a problem, and I suppose it's because both sides of my life give me energy. That's what I recommend to both interns and executives.

Here, Bezos does seem to nod towards the fact that he has a capacity for hard work that few can match among the general run of the population – his phrase 'maybe there are limits' suggests that Bezos finds it hard to understand those who have less workplace endurance. But the principal take-away from this passage is not that we should work tirelessly, but rather that we should buy into every aspect of life with the zeal of the 'missionary', using the interest in work and the love of home as fuels running from the same tank.

WEALTH AND PROSPERITY

Much has been made of Bezos' unimaginable wealth. The viewpoints come in from various angles, and often at polar opposites. Some, for example, view Bezos' wealth as an inspiration, the most tangible indicator of the way that Bezos has built success for himself and hundreds of thousands of employees. Seen through this lens, Bezos' wealth rubber stamps his greatness as an entrepreneur, investor and intellectual explorer. For others, by contrast, his wealth is something of a blot on the social fabric of humanity, a supreme example of the gross inequalities. Mind-blowing 'facts', some of them questionable or ignorant of the fact that much of Bezos' wealth is tied up in stock (which varies in value), abound on the internet, such as: Bezos makes more in a second than the median US worker makes in a week; every hour adds $8.9 million to his wealth; he is worth more than the GDP of 140 of the world's 195 countries. The accuracy of many of these facts is constantly up for change and re-evaluation, but we can certainly acknowledge that Bezos has achieved a financial status that few have done in human history.

What does this mean for Bezos personally? I think that it would be very difficult to argue that for Bezos wealth was *the* primary goal of all his endeavours. The relentless pace at which he has driven himself to the present day, and which he looks likely to sustain well into the future, indicates that he never had a vision of a financial arrival point at which he would slip his foot off the gas. For Bezos, the wealth generated is a tangible metric of the health and future-looking vitality of that business. He has stated explicitly that he has never sought the title of 'world's richest man', preferring instead to be noted for his work as an entrepreneur or inventor. In the same breath (in an interview for the Economic Club), he explained that his ownership of 16 per cent of Amazon stock, a $1 trillion company, means that $840 billion of wealth has been created for other people. Fixating on his personal wealth at the expense of acknowledging wealth generated for others skews the picture.

But as Bezos' personal wealth has grown, at first impressively, then stratospherically, he has become a lightning rod for controversy regarding the working conditions and pay of his employees, especially those on the lower rungs of the organizational charts. Bezos is not unaware of the nature of the disputes and arguments. In his 2019 letter to shareholders, he wrote a section titled 'Leveraging Scale for Good', in which he defended vigorously Amazon's record on employment, seen through the prism of scale. He explained how Amazon employed 840,000 workers around the world and 'directly or indirectly supported' another 2 million jobs in the

United States. Some 830,000 jobs were sustained by the businesses that made a living selling through Amazon. Taking everything together, Amazon supports more than 4 million workers around the world. Bezos also defensively homed in on the particulars of Amazon wages and benefits, pointing to the fact that Amazon's starting minimum wage of $15 per hour (implemented in 2018; today it is an average wage of more than $18 an hour, a figure adopted in 2021 in the face of the Covid-19-induced recruitment crisis) contrasted sharply with the federal minimum wage of $7.25 per hour. Bezos explained that Amazon was in the process of lobbying the US government to raise the federal minimum to match Amazon rates. He also pointed to Amazon US employee benefits – health insurance from day one, 20 weeks' paid parental leave, a 401(k) plan (a tax-advantageous retirement savings plan), across the company. It is evident from the granularity of the details here that Bezos was keen to defend his employee record with data.

The 'scale for good' has some further important logic that needs teasing out to appreciate Bezos' approach to management more fully. Bezos is, at heart, an entrepreneur. The landscape in which any entrepreneur operates is harsh and adversarial, with the odds stacked against success from the outset. Finding a way to survive, then stability, then growth and profit inculcates scrappy values that are hard to shed for the creator even when a business reaches massive scale. Bezos implicitly subscribes to a usefully succinct sentence in the Forbes.com article 'Why Is Scaling So Important In Business?' (31 October 2019), which summarizes the importance of scaling in a start-up business: 'Scaling is critical because sustainable growth tends to be the cure for everything else that can and does go wrong at a start-up.' What is significant in this statement is the idea that scaling up is not about greed or desire to ever conquer new commercial lands. Fundamentally, scaling up is to do with giving your start-up the capacity to survive the endless parade of mistakes, exceptional and fixed costs, competition, and the thousand other things that assail a new business. For Bezos, Amazon had to be run permanently on the aggression and passion of a start-up. He explains this in terms of a 'Day One' mentality:

> Since our founding, we have strived to maintain a 'Day One' mentality at the company. By that I mean approaching everything we do with the energy and entrepreneurial spirit of Day One. Even though Amazon is a large company, I have always believed that if we commit ourselves to maintaining a Day One mentality as a critical part of our DNA, we can have both the scope and capabilities of a large company and the spirit and heart of a small one.

The Day One mentality has achieved a certain fashionability in the world of business management theory, with many companies large and small attempting to incorporate the dynamic outlook into its corporate culture. But as many have discovered, this is far easier to say than it is to do. The Day One mentality requires that managers embrace characteristics that to Bezos appear as second nature, but to many managers are too uncomfortable to embrace with conviction – an elevated tolerance for high risk; a willingness to hire people who don't fit the traditional profiles of the position; significantly reducing unnecessary levels of communication; obsessively focusing on the customer; scaling up at the expense, temporarily, of profits; vigorously undermining one's own business model with a drive for innovation. Bezos also espouses that his Amazon 'missionaries' have two core qualities in permanent, simultaneous drive: stubbornness and flexibility:

> We are stubborn on vision. We are flexible on details ... We don't give up on things easily. Our third-party seller business is an example of that. It took us three tries to get the third-party seller business to work. We didn't give up ... If you're not stubborn, you'll give up on experiments too soon. And if you're not flexible, you'll pound your head against the wall and you won't see a different solution to a problem you're trying to solve.

Unflinchingly focused on the goal but constantly open to new ways of getting there – that appears to be the model Bezos employee.

For Bezos, the size or success of the company never alters the scrappiness needed to succeed in a competitive marketplace. If Bezos has an idea that will seize a market advantage, it is not enough simply to get the car rolling and then take your foot off the gas. Instead, the momentum of the advantage has to be maintained through growth; through this lens, the scale Amazon has achieved is simply applying start-up logic to continual scaling up, an ongoing need to put distance between you and your competition, even if that competition isn't visible (yet). Bezos here explains the advantage Amazon seized with AWS and other products and services:

> As soon as we hatched that plan for ourselves, it became immediately obvious that every company in the world was going to want this. What really surprised us was that thousands of developers flocked to these APIs without much promotion or fanfare from Amazon.

And then a business miracle that never happens happened—the greatest piece of business luck in the history of business, so far as I know. We faced no like-minded competition for seven years. It's unbelievable. When I launched Amazon.com in 1995, Barnes & Noble then launched Barnesandnoble.com and entered the market two years later in 1997. Two years later is very typical if you invent something new. We launched Kindle; Barnes & Noble launched Nook two years later. We launched Echo; Google launched Google Home two years later. When you pioneer, if you're lucky, you get a two-year head start. Nobody gets a seven-year head start, and so that was unbelievable.

For Bezos, it is crucial for a company to lead from the front rather than react from behind. Here, he lists several Amazon innovations that broke the mould and left others struggling to catch up.

LEGACY

Bringing together the threads outlined above, we perhaps view the criticisms levelled at Bezos in a more understandable light. In his world, without the focus on growth, delivered through a Day One outlook, all the hundreds of thousands of jobs that rest in the hands of Amazon and his other ventures could be at risk. That much might seem impossible, given the massive reach of Amazon today, but modern history is littered with multi-billion-dollar industries that slipped or crashed into bankruptcy (although some have since recovered) – WorldCom, Lehman Brothers, Pacific Gas and Electric, Borders, General Motors, Enron, Conseco, to name but a few. But Bezos has progressively discovered, as have many billionaire entrepreneurs, that the discipline, aggression and hard choices that deliver scale are rarely universally popular, and most such individuals at some point cross the invisible barrier from being lauded to being vilified. Bezos has kept his focus on scale, knowing that to do otherwise could result in costs greater than those incurred through pursuing it.

Whatever your perspective on Bezos as a man, there are very few indeed who could deny that he is a remarkable individual. His empire of achievement, sprawling out across commerce, books, TV, movies, philanthropy, space, and much more, can be traced back to his personal visions and hands-on efforts. By his own endeavours, he has changed the modern world.

The ultimate objective of any entrepreneur biography is not only to present the narrative of the individual in question, but also to give the reader a sense of the inner life at work, the psychological ghost in the corporate machine. In some ways, this is difficult to do with Bezos. He is rigorously controlled in the communications he sends out into the public domain – it is incredibly difficult to hear Bezos say anything off message when there is a microphone around. In this way, he might be showing a deep understanding of how the world now works around his celebrity, rather than just demonstrating he has had good media training. In the press conference following his flight on *New Shepard*, Bezos, building up to announce the launch of his new Courage and Civility Award, reflected on a wider problem of the digital age:

And really what we should always be doing is questioning ideas, not the person. Ad hominem attacks have been around a long time, but they don't work. And they've been amplified by social media. We need unifiers and not vilifiers. We want people who argue hard and act hard for what they truly believe, but they do that always with civility and never ad hominem attacks. And unfortunately, we live in a world where this is too often not the case. But we do have role models.

The words here seem particularly heartfelt, coming from a man whose life and every action has been under the most caustic scrutiny. The accounts of Bezos' character reveal a human being as flawed and mercurial as any other, prone to sudden anger (but equally, sudden decompression), noted for his outrageous, joyous laugh but also, on occasions, his intimidating presence, laser focused on technicalities but at times dismissive of any and all objections to an idea. But one true constant is that Bezos is always interested in ideas. It is those he would prefer the wider world to see.

SOURCES AND FURTHER READING

The sources for quotations from Jeff Bezos himself come from a collection of his writings, press releases, social media postings and interviews. The following in particular should be referenced (all such quotations are the copyright of Jeff Bezos):

Letters to shareholders, 1997–2020

Amazon press release archive: https://press.aboutamazon.com/press-releases

Blue Origin news archive: www.blueorigin.com/news-archive

Blue Origin post-flight press conference, 20 July 2021: www.youtube.com/watch?v=qVBmyqhmt20

Bezos Expeditions website (includes statements and press releases relating to Blue Origin, the *Washington Post*, Bezos Day One Fund, Bezos Family Foundation, 10,000 Year Clock, F-1 Engine Recovery and 'Selected Investments'): www.bezosexpeditions.com/

Jeff Bezos Twitter: https://twitter.com/JeffBezos

Jeff Bezos Instagram: www.instagram.com/jeffbezos/

Interviews given at The Economic Club Of Washington: www.youtube.com/c/TheEconomicClubofWashingtonDC

Interviews for the Reagan National Defense Forum: www.reaganfoundation.org/reagan-institute/programs/reagan-

national-defense-forum/ and www.youtube.com/channel/
UCEJi23qnygQHE5UeLXoV_JQ

Interview between Mark and Jeff Bezos, 4 November 2017: www.
youtube.com/watch?v=Hq89wYzOjfs

Interview for the Ignatius Forum, 'Our Future in Space', 10 November
2021: www.youtube.com/watch?v=UWyPk_f8aAA

The Climate Pledge launch conference, 19 September 2019, Amazon
News: www.youtube.com/watch?v=oz9iO0EOpI0

Princeton University's 2010 Baccalaureate address: www.youtube.com/
watch?v=Duml1SHJqNE

Interview for *Montessori Life*, Winter 2000 issue: https://gallery.
mailchimp.com/0e28a613cf5e40a5c7a457727/files/b9164cd0-
a5cb-454b-97dc-79f963e1bdc8/Jeff_Bezos_Montessori_Life_
Winter_2000.pdf

Speech given at COP26 climate summit in Glasgow, United Kingdom, 2
November 2021: www.youtube.com/watch?v=6NKctlp7yY0

SELECTED FURTHER READING

Afil, Raphael, *Jeff Bezos: In His Own Words* (Raphael Afil, 2021)

Amazon Leadership Principles: www.amazon.jobs/en-gb/principles

Amazon Web Services Whitepapers and Guides: https://aws.amazon.
com/whitepapers/

Bezos, Jeff, *Invent and Wander: The Collected Writings of Jeff Bezos*
(Boston, MA, Harvard Business Review Press, 2021)

Brandt, Richard L., *One Click: Jeff Bezos and the Rise of Amazon*
(London, Penguin, 2012)

Bryar, Colin, *Working Backwards: Insights, Stories, and Secrets from
Inside Amazon* (London, Macmillan, 2021)

Christensen, Clayton M., *The Innovator's Dilemma: When New Technologies Cause Great Firms to Fail* (Boston, MA, Harvard Business Review Press, 2016)

Collins, Jim, *Good to Great: Why Some Companies Make the Leap … and Others Don't* (London, Harper Business, 2011)

Cook, John, 'Meet Amazon.com's first employee: Shel Kaphan', GeekWire.com (14 June 2011): www.geekwire.com/2011/meet-shel-kaphan-amazoncom-employee-1/

Currier, James, 'The CEO That Jeff Bezos Called "His Teacher"', NfX. com: www.nfx.com/post/the-ceo-that-jeff-bezos-called-his-teacher/ (accessed 28 February 2022)

Davenport, Christian, *The Space Barons: Elon Musk, Jeff Bezos, and the Quest to Colonize the Cosmos* (New York, Hachette, 2019)

Del Valle, Gaby, 'Jeff Bezos's philanthropic projects aren't as generous as they seem'. Vox.com (29 November 2018): www.vox.com/the-goods/2018/11/29/18116720/jeff-bezos-day-1-fund-homelessness

Döpfner, Mathias, 'Jeff Bezos reveals what it's like to build an empire — and why he's willing to spend $1 billion a year to fund the most important mission of his life', Businessinsider.com (28 April 2018): www.businessinsider.com/jeff-bezos-interview-axel-springer-ceo-amazon-trump-blue-origin-family-regulation-washington-post-2018-4?r=US&IR=T

SpaceNews.com articles relating to Blue Origin: https://spacenews.com

Stone, Brad, *The Everything Store: Jeff Bezos and the Age of Amazon* (London, Penguin-Random House, 2018)

Stone, Brad, *Amazon Unbound: Jeff Bezos and the Invention of a Global Empire* (New York and London, Simon & Schuster, 2021)

INDEX